first 15

Printed in Dallas, Texas by The Odee Company

Contact: contact@first15.org
www.first15.org

Designed by Matt Ravenelle
mattravenelle.com

ABOUT FIRST15

Spending time alone with God every day can be a struggle. We're busier – and more stressed – than ever. But still, we know it's important to spend time alone with our Creator. We know we need to read his word, pray, and worship him.

First15 bridges the gap between desire and reality, helping you establish the rhythm of meaningful, daily experiences in God's presence. First15 answers the critical questions:

• Why should I spend time alone with God?
• How do I spend time alone with God?
• How do I get the most out of my time alone with God?
• How can I become more consistent with my time alone with God?

And by answering these questions through the format of daily devotionals, you'll practice the rhythm of meeting with God while experiencing the incredible gift of his loving presence given to those who make time to meet with him.

Allow God's passionate pursuit to draw you in across the next several days. And watch as every day is better than the last as your life is built on the solid foundation of God's love through the power of consistent, meaningful time alone with him.

To learn more about First15, visit our website first15. org. First15 is available across mobile app, email, podcast, and our website. Subscribe to our devotional today and experience God in a fresh way every day.

———————

ABOUT THE AUTHOR

Craig Denison is the author of First15, a daily devotional guiding over a million believers into a fresh experience with God every day. In 2015, Craig founded First15 after sensing a longing in God's heart for his people to be about relationship – real, restored relationship with him – that above all else, he simply wanted the hearts of his people. Craig began praying, dreaming, and writing. And the idea of helping people spend the first fifteen minutes of their day focusing on nothing else but growing in their relationship with God was born. The vision was birthed in Craig's heart that if we as a people would worship, read, and pray at the beginning of every day, everything could change for the better. Craig writes, speaks, and he and his wife, Rachel lead worship to help believers establish a more tangible, meaningful connection with God.

––––––––

CONTENTS

Grace

"For by grace you have been saved through faith. And this is not your own doing; it is the gift of God, not a result of works, so that no one may boast." Ephesians 2:8-9

WEEKLY OVERVIEW

Grace is a gift most of us don't know how to receive. We've been so inundated with the earthly systems of give-and-get and work-and-earn that grace is a concept few ever fully grasp. Yet it's grace alone that has the power to transform lives. Grace alone has the power to bring freedom to the captives. By grace alone we are saved. There could be no better use of our time than consistently and passionately pursuing a greater revelation of God's grace.

DEVOTIONAL

It seems like every day I discover new ways in which I am weak and in need. Whether it be sin, physical exhaustion, or emotional dependence, I am constantly discovering my need for help. But daily I also discover a God who is wholly sufficient in all the ways I am weak. Daily I receive rejuvenation from my heavenly Father who seems to take these weaknesses of mine and use them for his kingdom.

Paul writes in 2 Corinthians 12:9, *"But [God] said to me, 'My grace is sufficient for you, for my power is made perfect in weakness.' Therefore I will boast all the more gladly of my weaknesses, so that the power of Christ may rest upon me."* What great comfort we can find in the words of Paul here. And what amazing love our heavenly Father has for us that he would bestow his sufficient grace upon us.

We serve a God who turns our greatest weakness into our greatest strength. In his grace, all he asks of us is to have a heart open, willing, and receptive to him. Our God is one who comes down to us and lays

down his life that we might live through him. He's the King of Kings who washes the feet of the very men who would betray him. He's the God of compassion who heals the sick and spends time with the sinners rather than the pious. He has given up any form of personal gain in order to devote his entire existence to paving the way for us to have restored relationship with our heavenly Father.

We serve a God whose grace is wholly sufficient for us. In fact, it's only in living by his grace that we are made strong. Your heavenly Father says, *"My power is made perfect in weakness."* In Christ we can boast in our need for our need is our greatest asset. Christ demonstrated through his ministry that he works powerfully when people simply acknowledge their need of him. From the woman desperate to touch his garment, to Zacchaeus the tax collector, to the paralyzed man lowered through the ceiling, God works incredible miracles in the lives of those who come before him with all their brokenness and need. His power is made perfect in those who simply cry out to him in desperation.

"But he said to me, 'My grace is sufficient for you, for my power is made perfect in weakness.' Therefore I will boast all the more gladly of my weaknesses, so that the power of Christ may rest upon me."

2 CORINTHIANS 12:9

In contrast, we see those in Scripture who come before God thinking they have it all, and therefore receive nothing from him. Mark 10:17-27 tells us of a rich, young ruler who came to Jesus asking for his help but was unwilling to trade worldly success for eternal relationship. In response to the young man's unwillingness Jesus says, *"How difficult it will be for those who have wealth to enter the kingdom of God!"* (Mark 10:23). I don't believe Jesus was just talking about monetary wealth here, although money is most definitely included. I believe Jesus is making a statement about anyone who feels satisfied in themselves and the world apart from God. You can be poor and still receive nothing from God because you live pridefully without acknowledging your need. One of our greatest gifts is weakness because in acknowledging our weakness we make space for God to move and work. Those who are satisfied with worldly success, pleasure, and possession make little room for the incredible wealth of love, peace, passion, and joy God longs to give those who simply acknowledge their need of him.

You see, this life is not about possession, whether it be little or much—it's about the posture of your heart toward God. The abundant life God longs to give you will only be received in areas where you acknowledge your weakness and need. The thief hanging on the cross who acknowledged his own sin received the gift of eternal life, not the pious and successful high priest who, in his pride, fought to crucify the very Savior he had been asking to come.

Posture your heart today as all those who have received the incredible wealth of the Lord's love have before you. Ask the Spirit to show you your dependence and need of God if you don't already know it. Ask God to humble you and make you receptive to all he longs to give. May it be his grace that is sufficient for you today, rather than your own strength. May it be his power that proves strong in your weakness. And may you experience today all the sufficient grace your heavenly Father longs to give.

13

GUIDED PRAYER

1. Reflect on your own need of God. Ask the Spirit to reveal to you your weakness. Spend time acknowledging your own sin, selfishness, pride and brokenness.

"But he said to me, 'My grace is sufficient for you, for my power is made perfect in weakness.' Therefore I will boast all the more gladly of my weaknesses, so that the power of Christ may rest upon me." 2 Corinthians 12:9

2. Receive the grace God longs to give you. Spend time receiving his love and enjoyment over you. Receive the love, forgiveness, joy, and peace your heavenly Father longs to pour out on the broken and needy places of your heart.

"He heals the brokenhearted and binds up their wounds." Psalm 147:3

3. Ask God to move in power through your life today. Ask him to guide and help you accomplish what is set before you today through the power of the Spirit.

"I can do all things through him who strengthens me." Philippians 4:13

No matter how gifted you are, God will always work through you to greater levels than you could accomplish on your own. Surrender your life to him and allow him to lead you to a lifetime of his unmerited favor. Every day as you wake up, acknowledge your dependence on God that your day may be lived in the abundance available to you. There is no better prayer you could pray in the morning than one asking God for his love, grace, and power in acknowledgement of your need of him.

Extended Reading: Matthew 5:1-12

DEVOTIONAL

We live in a world built on transaction. We give and we get. We only receive what we earn or deserve. We're hired and fired based on our abilities and performance. We commit our lives to this system of cause and effect, relishing the days of success and wincing at the thought of failure. And often as believers we take this system of works we've grown so comfortable with and apply it to our relationship with God. We operate with God much like we operate with an employer. We think if we can go to church, give God our money, spend enough time with him in the morning, be happy, and help people, then God will like us. If we can stop sinning, then God will love us more. But God's ways are not like ours. The New Testament names this transactional relationship with God as living under the law and tells us of a new system through Christ called grace.

God established the law as a system for his people to be cleansed through sacrifice. For thousands of years God's holiness required his children to pay a price for their sin in order to be in relationship with him. Sin separated us from our heavenly Father like a cell wall separating a prisoner from freedom. Our only hope for guidance and love was living by the commands of our just and holy God, and we failed miserably. So grace stepped in where works could never prevail. Galatians 4:4-7 says:

"The sting of death is sin, and the power of sin is the law. But thanks be to God, who gives us the victory through our Lord Jesus Christ."

1 CORINTHIANS 15:56-57

When the fullness of time had come, God sent forth his Son, born of woman, born under the law, to redeem those who were under the law, so that we might receive adoption as sons. And because you are sons, God has sent the Spirit of his Son into our hearts, crying, "Abba! Father!" So you are no longer a slave, but a son, and if a son, then an heir through God.

Jesus lived the perfect life none of us could, and then offered himself as the final and resounding sacrifice, buying freedom for all who would believe in him. He saved you and me from the law and offers us grace.

But still we persist in paying the penalty for our own sin as if the death of Jesus wasn't enough. Still we choose a transactional relationship over one of grace. But what we often don't understand is how foundational grace is to freedom from sin. 1 Corinthians 15:56-57 says, *"The sting of death is sin, and the power of sin is the law. But thanks be to God, who gives us the victory through our Lord Jesus Christ."* When we live under the law we are bound by sin and separated from victory in Christ. And Romans 6:14 says, *"For sin will have no dominion over you, since you are not under law but under grace."* It's by living in grace that we experience continual freedom from sin. In our own strength we are powerless against the schemes of the enemy. But in God's grace

we live by his strength. In acknowledging our need of God's grace and help, we live by the power of God.

You see, we are meant to be fueled for freedom by the unconditional love of our heavenly Father. He offers grace-filled love to guide us out of the systems of this world. It's the power of restored relationship that lays the foundation for us to choose satisfaction in him over the world. Galatians 5:1 says, *"For freedom Christ has set us free; stand firm therefore, and do not submit again to a yoke of slavery."* You are no longer enslaved to the law. Christ has set you free. So you have to choose to submit to the life of grace you've been offered. You have to choose to live in light of God's power working in you instead of leaning on your own works to get you through. You have to choose to acknowledge your weakness to receive the strength his grace offers you.

Free yourself from the bondage of living life in your own strength. Cast off the chains of pride that bind you to a lifestyle of sin and receive a fresh revelation of the unconditional love of God. Your heavenly Father loves you simply because he loves you. There is nothing you can do that will make him love you more, and there is nothing you can do that will make him love you less. Allow his grace-filled love to transform your heart today and guide you into a life of freedom.

17

GUIDED PRAYER

1. Meditate on the importance of living under grace instead of works.

"The sting of death is sin, and the power of sin is the law. But thanks be to God, who gives us the victory through our Lord Jesus Christ." 1 Corinthians 15:56-57

"For sin will have no dominion over you, since you are not under law but under grace." Romans 6:14

2. Confess any ways in which you've been pursuing relationship with God through works. Have you had any thoughts of needing to do something or be something to gain his affections and approval? Have you veiled your heart in any way as the result of sin or misunderstanding?

3. Choose today to live a life free from sin under the power of grace. Lean on him for guidance and power. Acknowledge your weakness and receive the strength that comes from the Holy Spirit weaving the story of grace into every page of your heart.

May you receive the peace that can come only from living your life in total submission to God. Pride will only burden you. Trying to prove to yourself and others that you have what it takes will only bring failure, frustration, and sin. As a desire to elevate yourself creeps back into your heart, remind yourself of where the paths of law and grace take you. Choose to live your life in response to God's grace, work out of the revelation that you are already loved, and discover newfound freedom from sin.

Extended Reading: 1 Corinthians 15

The Throne of Grace

DAY 3

DEVOTIONAL

What do you picture in your mind's eye when I talk about God sitting on his throne? I always picture a massive throne with tiny little me staring up at a distant face feeling about the size of God's pinky toe. The idea of a throne makes God seem too large to be near to me, as if he was too big to notice me.

There is Scripture that speaks about how large and majestic God is on his throne, to be sure! Isaiah 6:1 says, *"In the year that King Uzziah died I saw the Lord sitting upon a throne, high and lifted up; and the train*

> *"Let us then with confidence draw near to the*
> *throne of grace, that we may receive mercy*
> *and find grace to help in time of need."*

of his robe filled the temple." And Revelation 20:11 says, *"Then I saw a great white throne and him who was seated on it. From his presence earth and sky fled away, and no place was found for them."*

Seemingly in contrast to the previous ideas, Hebrews 4:16 says, *"Let us then with confidence draw near to the throne of grace, that we may receive mercy and find grace to help in time of need."* After reading Hebrews 4:16, I get a completely different picture of God on his throne. Hebrews paints for us a picture of a throne of grace rather than a distant ruler. It speaks of a throne from which comes mercy and help for those in need. And it commands us to come before the throne of the King of Kings, Creator and Ruler of all, with confidence. Hebrews 4:16 makes me love how huge God is on his throne because the bigger he is, the more grace and mercy there is.

Your God is full of both power and compassion. His presence brings both fear and grace. He is a God whose voice both commands obedience and is full of the richest kind of love. And he is beckoning you to draw near to him today so that he can offer you grace, mercy, and help.

James 4:8 tells us, *"Draw near to God, and he will draw near to you."* The same God whose robe fills the temple longs for you as his child to simply get wrapped up in his arms. You can boldly come before the Lord of Lords and tell him all of your needs. David understood this when he wrote in Psalm 40:17, *"As for me, I am poor and needy, but the Lord takes thought for me. You are my help and my deliverer; do not delay, O my God!"* And Jesus teaches us in Matthew 7:7-11:

Ask, and it will be given to you; seek, and you will find; knock, and it will be opened to you. For everyone who asks receives, and the one who seeks finds, and to the one who knocks it will be opened. Or which one of you, if his son asks him for bread, will give him a stone? Or if he asks for a fish, will give him a serpent? If you then, who are evil, know how to give good gifts to your children, how much more will your Father who is in heaven give good things to those who ask him!

So where do you need God's help today? Where do you need his mercy and grace in your life? Know that he is not a God who is distant but one who is closer than your own heartbeat. He's a God who knows all and is full of love and mercy. He's a Father who gives the best gifts to his children. Whatever you have need of today, come before the throne of grace and boldly ask for it. If you hunger for righteousness, you will be satisfied. If you need provision, God has promised to take care of your every need. Your heavenly Father loves you and longs to bless you with every good and perfect gift.

21

GUIDED PRAYER

1. Renew your mind to God's incredible gift of grace.

"Let us then with confidence draw near to the throne of grace, that we may receive mercy and find grace to help in time of need." Hebrews 4:16

2. Ask God for whatever need you have. What do you have need of? Where do you need God's help?

"Ask, and it will be given to you; seek, and you will find; knock, and it will be opened to you. For everyone who asks receives, and the one who seeks finds, and to the one who knocks it will be opened. Or which one of you, if his son asks him for bread, will give him a stone? Or if he asks for a fish, will give him a serpent? If you then, who are evil, know how to give good gifts to your children, how much more will your Father who is in heaven give good things to those who ask him!" Matthew 7:7-11

3. Come before the throne of God with confidence and receive the help he desires to give you. Draw near to him, and let his presence satisfy your need for love, forgiveness, and attention.

"Draw near to God, and he will draw near to you." James 4:8

Whenever you need help today you can run with confidence to your heavenly Father's throne room. Take time throughout your day and ask for his help. If the enemy attacks with temptation, come before the throne of grace and allow God to satisfy you. If you come up against a wall, ask God to show you how to conquer it! He is with you always, and he longs to help you in his limitless grace and love for you. Don't live your life today as if God wasn't right there with you. Seek his help in every situation and follow his leadership in whatever way he provides it.

Extended Reading: Hebrews 4

DEVOTIONAL

The most gracious gift God continues to give us as his children is his presence. Moses writes a beautiful and powerful prayer in Numbers 6:25: *"The Lord make his face to shine upon you and be gracious to you."* Rest in the sweet imagery of that prayer for a moment. Reflect on the goodness of having God's face shine upon you. Feel the peace that comes from God's graciousness.

There is nothing better in life than encountering God because it's only in his presence that we are truly satisfied. Scripture illustrates this truth in Psalm 84 when the Psalmist writes:

For a day in your courts is better than a thousand elsewhere. I would rather be a doorkeeper in the house of my God than dwell in the tents of wickedness. For the

"The Lord make his face to shine
upon you and be gracious to you."

Lord God is a sun and shield; the Lord bestows favor and honor. No good thing does he withhold from those who walk uprightly. O Lord of hosts, blessed is the one who trusts in you!

To encounter God is to experience his goodness. To spend time in his presence is to experience the very *"favor and honor"* that only comes from his nearness.

What would it be like to live your life entirely in the presence of God? What would change if you were to experience his goodness with every moment, waking or sleeping? How would the reality of his presence change the way you live your life for the better? The remarkable thing is that we have no reason to live our lives apart from God. When Jesus died, God tore the veil from top to bottom that separated us from him. His tearing of the veil symbolizes the entire reason for the death of Jesus: that God can once again dwell among his people. And furthermore, when you became a Christian you were filled with God himself. He's closer to you than the very breath that fills your lungs.

You see, it's by God's grace that we have his presence. It's by his love that he makes himself near to us. God's word tells us we can never escape his presence. Psalm 139:9-10 says, *"If I take the wings of the morning and dwell in the uttermost parts of the sea, even there your hand shall lead me, and your right hand shall hold me."* Acts 17:27-28 says, *"Yet he is actually not far from each one of us, for 'In him we live and move and have our being.'"* Your greatest gift is always available to you. No matter where you turn, God will be there. No sin can separate you from his presence because his presence comes to you by grace, not by your works. So great is God's love for you that he offers you his gracious presence regardless of anything you do, right or wrong.

All that is required of you is to open your heart and receive the gift he offers. There is an endless amount of God's presence to receive. He is a vast and endless ocean that will never be fully discovered. But still he calls you to come and dive in. The Bible commands us in Ephesians 5:18 to *"be filled with the Spirit,"* to be filled with God himself. This passage is better translated, *"Be being filled."* God asks us to constantly be filled with his presence because he knows it is our greatest gift. And the death of Christ has paved the way for us to receive this gift constantly.

Spend time today simply being filled with God's presence offered to you by his grace. May you experience the *"favor and honor"* that can only be found by resting in the presence of your heavenly Father.

GUIDED PRAYER

1. Meditate on Scripture about God's presence. Renew your mind to the fact that he is with you right now and that his presence is your greatest gift.

"For a day in your courts is better than a thousand elsewhere. I would rather be a doorkeeper in the house of my God than dwell in the tents of wickedness. For the Lord God is a sun and shield; the Lord bestows favor and honor. No good thing does he withhold from those who walk uprightly. O Lord of hosts, blessed is the one who trusts in you!" Psalm 84:10-12

2. Receive God's presence. Open your heart and ask him to come near to you. Take note of how you feel different in response to his presence.

"Draw near to God, and he will draw near to you." James 4:8

"But for me it is good to be near God; I have made the Lord God my refuge, that I may tell of all your works." Psalm 73:28

3. Live today in the continual presence of your heavenly Father. If you notice yourself living outside of the nearness of God, just take a minute and receive his presence again.

"If I take the wings of the morning and dwell in the uttermost parts of the sea, even there your hand shall lead me, and your right hand shall hold me." Psalm 139:9-10

"Yet he is actually not far from each one of us, for 'In him we live and move and have our being.'" Acts 17:27-28

As you go out today in pursuit of the presence of God, keep this quote from Brother Lawrence close to your heart. May it fuel you toward the goodness and simplicity of encountering your heavenly Father in all that you do.

"He does not ask much of us, merely a thought of Him from time to time, a little act of adoration, sometimes to ask for His grace, sometimes to offer Him your sufferings, at other times to thank Him for the graces, past and present, He has bestowed on you, in the midst of your troubles to take solace in Him as often as you can. Lift up your heart to Him during your meals and in company; the least little remembrance will always be the most pleasing to Him. One need not cry out very loudly; He is nearer to us than we think (Practicing the Presence of God)."

Extended Reading: Psalm 84

DEVOTIONAL

We are the children of a heavenly Father who richly provides everything we need to live, love, and work according to the perfect plans he has for us. Matthew 6:26 beautifully illustrates God's promise of provision. Jesus says, *"Look at the birds of the air: they neither sow nor reap nor gather into barns, and yet your heavenly Father feeds them. Are you not of more value than they?"* The earth clearly demonstrates God's ability to provide for his creation. He gives rain to the grass of the field and trees of the forest. Then as quickly

*"As for the rich in this present age, charge
them not to be haughty, nor to set their hopes
on the uncertainty of riches, but on God, who
richly provides us with everything to enjoy."*

1 TIMOTHY 6:17

as the clouds come, he rolls them away to bring life-giving sunshine to all of creation. And Jesus' statement in Matthew 6 makes it clear: we are of far more value to God than any other part of creation. We are of such value to God that he sent his only son Jesus to pay the highest price of an unjust death that we might be able to live an abundant and new life through him.

God provides for us both spiritually and physically because of the abundant grace he has for us. 1 Timothy 6:17 says, *"As for the rich in this present age, charge them not to be haughty, nor to set their hopes on the uncertainty of riches, but on God, who richly provides us with everything to enjoy."* It's his grace that drives him to richly bless us even though we deserve nothing. His grace drives him to give us every good gift—not our own works. And because of God's grace, we can place our hope in him for complete provision with full assurance that his promises will come to pass.

1 Timothy 6:17 clearly illustrates a separation between putting our hope in God and putting hope in ourselves or the world. Too often we miss the fact that everything we have was given to us by the grace of God. And in doing so we allow the belief that we've earned what we've received to creep into our hearts, resulting in a feeling of entitlement rather than thanksgiving.

Entitlement is a disease that's spread decay and death too far throughout the body of Christ. It kills any area in which it is allowed to enter by leading us to a life of pride and selfishness rather than hope and joy. It enslaves us to ourselves, as if we somehow deserve possession, status, power, friendship, or authority. When we don't see everything we've received as a gift by God's grace, we live our lives constantly toiling and striving to earn what our heavenly Father has already promised to give us. And when we have failures or problems, we alone carry the burden of need rather than looking to our faithful heavenly Father as our provider.

This life is not about what we have, but relationship with the God who has provided for us. If God has blessed you abundantly in the area of provision, I pray that you use every single possession as another opportunity to give thanks to the God who provided it for you in his grace. Every talent, skill, and dollar you possess was given to you because you are the child of a Father who loves you more deeply than you will ever know. All of us have been richly blessed by a God who faithfully provides for us. May we all walk in the freedom that comes as we live with the hope of God as our sole provider. May we see everything God uses to provide for us as a wonderful gift given to us by our heavenly Father. And may we serve and love God alone as we live our lives free from the slavery of pursuing the world.

GUIDED PRAYER

1. Meditate on God's provision. Allow Scripture to transform your belief about who or what is providing for you.

"As for the rich in this present age, charge them not to be haughty, nor to set their hopes on the uncertainty of riches, but on God, who richly provides us with everything to enjoy." 1 Timothy 6:17

"Look at the birds of the air: they neither sow nor reap nor gather into barns, and yet your heavenly Father feeds them. Are you not of more value than they?" Matthew 6:26

"And my God will supply every need of yours according to his riches in glory in Christ Jesus." Philippians 4:19

2. Now reflect on your own heart. What do you feel enslaved to today? What job, person, or opportunity do you feel has become your master? Where do you feel the pain of entitlement rather than the freedom of a grace-filled perspective?

3. Confess to God any job, person, or opportunity you've been serving above him. Give over to him any way in which you've been living for your own gain rather than relationship with him. As you confess to God, allow his Spirit to break the chains that have been enslaving you to the world and its principles.

The world constantly attempts to enslave us. It tries to convince us that we need what it has and that it will satisfy our needs. But God's word and our experience clearly show that the world apart from God only brings pain and dissatisfaction. Proverbs 23:4-5 commands us, *"Do not toil to acquire wealth; be discerning enough to desist. When your eyes light on it, it is gone, for suddenly it sprouts wings, flying like an eagle toward heaven."* Satisfaction in the world comes and goes as quickly as an eagle flies across our view. May you find the peace and joy that comes from living your life in total freedom from the world. And may you experience rejuvenated hope and joy that can only come from serving God as your sole Lord and provider.

Extended Reading: Matthew 6

31

God's Grace Brings Purpose

DAY 6

DEVOTIONAL

One of the greatest gifts we've been given by God is purpose. From the time of Adam, God has always made clear the purposes we were created for. In Genesis 1:28 God says, *"Be fruitful and multiply and fill the earth and subdue it and have dominion over the fish of the sea and over the birds of the heavens and over every living thing that moves on the earth."* Throughout time our purposes have changed, but God has made it clear that we all are to have lives that are valuable and effective. Have you lived days where you're simply going through the motions? Have you had days where you feel as if what you do doesn't matter? Those days in my life are my absolute worst. I would rather go through trial and persecution with purpose than live a meaningless day. It's in purpose we find satisfaction. In purpose we find out our lives matter. And in purpose we discover the reason we were created.

2 Timothy 1:9 says, *"[God] saved us and called us to a holy calling, not because of our works but because of his own purpose and grace, which he gave us in Christ Jesus before the ages began."* Because of God's grace and purpose we have been called to a life of wonderful and satisfying works. The Bible teaches us a truth in opposition to the teachings of the world. The world says to work enough to live a life of comfort and ease. Work is done for the purpose of relaxation and comfort. God says that we are created for a life of eternal value in which everything we do is to have purpose higher than our own comfort and relaxation. God has placed value and worth on your life to an extent you have yet to discover. He has a plan and purpose for your life that he's assigned to no one else. Your life is meant to make an eternal impact for his kingdom which will reign for all time. But in his grace he has also given you control of your own life. You can choose to live your life according to his purposes or your own. And you can choose to pursue comfort and meaningless relaxation or a life of true rest and satisfaction that comes only from living entirely for God. My hope is that in looking at two purposes God has for your life, you will choose to live your life completely with and for your heavenly Father. And in doing so, you will discover the incredible joy and passion the Spirit longs to birth in you.

The first purpose for which you were created is relationship with God. Jesus says in Mark 12:30, *"And you shall love the Lord your God with all your heart and*

calling, not because of our works but because of his own purpose and grace, which he gave us in Christ Jesus before the ages began."

2 TIMOTHY 1:9

with all your soul and with all your mind and with all your strength." The Westminster Shorter Catechism says it this way: "The chief end of man is to glorify God and to enjoy Him forever." Loving God is your highest calling, and in loving God you will experience the fullest joy and satisfaction available. When you stand before God in judgment, he will not look for possessions, promotions, or social status, but rather at the fervor with which you loved him. You will be rewarded for acts of love, not self-seeking glorification. And this chief purpose of loving God is the only path to the abundant life he has in store for you here.

The second purpose for which you were created is loving others in response to your love for God. Mark 12:31 says, *"You shall love your neighbor as yourself."* Ephesians 5:1-2 says, *"Therefore be imitators of God, as beloved children. And walk in love, as Christ loved us and gave himself up for us, a fragrant offering and sacrifice to God."* Acts 26:16 says, *"But rise and stand upon your feet, for I have appeared to you for this purpose, to appoint you as a servant and witness to the things in which you have seen me and to those in which I will appear to you."* We are called to love others out of the amazing love we've been shown. As our hearts are filled with love for God through encountering him in the secret place, we will be filled with a longing to see his desires for others around us come to fruition. God's greatest longing is for relationship with his crown of creation, and he wants to use us to guide others to himself. In loving others we will discover the incredible satisfaction of seeing the lost and hurting be found and healed. Incredible passion and joy comes from seeing a life transformed through the Spirit working in us.

How incredible is the grace of our God that his purposes would be entirely rooted in love. We are called to simply love him and others with the very love we've been shown. He's like a father who gives his children money to buy him a present. He fills us with the love and enjoyment he feels for us, and then in response we can love him and others. He fills you with the breath of life and then patiently waits for you to live your life as a beautiful song of worship to him. May you experience today all that God's grace has afforded you. May you choose to live your life with purpose and passion that only comes from loving him and others.

33

GUIDED PRAYER

1. Meditate on God's desire to lead you to a life of abundant purpose.

"[God] saved us and called us to a holy calling, not because of our works but because of his own purpose and grace, which he gave us in Christ Jesus before the ages began." 2 Timothy 1:9

"You did not choose me, but I chose you and appointed you that you should go and bear fruit and that your fruit should abide." John 15:16

2. Reflect on your own life. Where have you been living with the purposes of the world rather than God? In what areas are you living for yourself rather than him and others? And in what areas of your life do you feel meaningless and passionless?

3. Receive the rejuvenation that comes from living with his purposes as your chief goals. Allow God to revive relationships that seem tired and passionless. Allow God to fill you with desire for your work, friendships, or marriage. Ask for the Spirit to reveal specific ways he desires to use you today.

The passion and purpose God has for you never ceases. There will be days or seasons he leads you to rest for the purpose of renewing, loving, and filling you. There will be times of work and striving in which he purposes to mold, shape, and use you. Wherever God is leading you today, trust that he absolutely has the best plan for you. Choose to live your life with his purposes in your heart and experience the passion that can only be found in living for God.

Extended Reading: Mark 12

In Grace God Teaches Us

DEVOTIONAL

By God's grace we have been given an entire book of his teaching. The Bible offers you practical wisdom, insight, and revelation that has the power to transform your life. Its very pages are miraculous, the voice of God breaking supernaturally into the physical world—paper and ink in your own language.

Matthew 24:35 says, *"Heaven and earth will pass away, but my words will not pass away."* The Bible holds the perfect and eternal words of the Creator of heaven and earth. Even more, as believers we've been filled with the very Author of the Bible, the Holy Spirit. We have available to us by God's grace both the word and its Author, capable together of leading us to the abundant life God desires for us. Today as we look at all that God desires to accomplish in us through his word, may your

"All Scripture is breathed out by God and profitable for teaching, for reproof, for correction, and for training in righteousness, that the man of God may be competent, equipped for every good work."

heart be filled with the longing to engage in the process of transformation that comes through the teaching of Scripture. Psalm 19:7-11 says:

The law of the Lord is perfect, reviving the soul; the testimony of the Lord is sure, making wise the simple; the precepts of the Lord are right, rejoicing the heart; the commandment of the Lord is pure, enlightening the eyes; the fear of the Lord is clean, enduring forever; the rules of the Lord are true, and righteous altogether. More to be desired are they than gold, even much fine gold; sweeter also than honey and drippings of the honeycomb. Moreover, by them is your servant warned; in keeping them there is great reward.

David understood the incredible value of the word he'd been given. God's word revives the soul, brings wisdom, rejoices the heart, and enlightens those who read it. How greatly do you need what God's word gives you? Where do you need to be revived? Where do you need wisdom, rejoicing, and enlightenment?

Psalm 1:1-3 says, *"Blessed is the man who walks not in the counsel of the wicked, nor stands in the way of sinners, nor sits in the seat of scoffers; but his delight is in the law of the Lord, and on his law he meditates day and night. He is like a tree planted by streams of water that yields its fruit in its season, and its leaf does not wither. In all that he does, he prospers."* Those who make God's word their

foundation and delight are immovable, fruitful, and prosperous. It has the power to lead you away from a life of sin and worldly counsel to a life of abundance and prosperity in the counsel of the Spirit.

2 Timothy 3:16-17 says, *"All Scripture is breathed out by God and profitable for teaching, for reproof, for correction, and for training in righteousness, that the man of God may be competent, equipped for every good work."* The Bible is capable of taking a broken, weak, and useless man and teaching, correcting, and training him in righteousness that he might be equipped for incredible works. God desires to take any area of your life that isn't yielding the fruit of righteousness or accomplishing good works and revive them through his word into areas of strength and life.

Because your heavenly Father loves you, he will always lead you through the Spirit and his word into better and more fruitful living. God has incredible plans in store for you as you grow in your relationship with him, and he desires to use his word to both equip you for and guide you to the abundant life he has for you. Meditate on his word day and night. Read it with the guidance of the Spirit. Receive the revelation, wisdom, and insight he longs to share with you. And choose to live your life in response to Scripture, living in obedience to all that you read.

GUIDED PRAYER

1. Meditate on all that God wants to do in you through his word.

"All Scripture is breathed out by God and profitable for teaching, for reproof, for correction, and for training in righteousness, that the man of God may be competent, equipped for every good work." 2 Timothy 3:16-17

"Blessed is the man who walks not in the counsel of the wicked, nor stands in the way of sinners, nor sits in the seat of scoffers; but his delight is in the law of the Lord, and on his law he meditates day and night. He is like a tree planted by streams of water that yields its fruit in its season, and its leaf does not wither. In all that he does, he prospers." Psalm 1:1-3

"The mouth of the righteous utters wisdom, and his tongue speaks justice. The law of his God is in his heart; his steps do not slip." Psalm 37:30-31

2. Reflect on your own life. Where do you need transformation? Where do you need restoration? Where do you need wisdom?

"The law of the Lord is perfect, reviving the soul; the testimony of the Lord is sure, making wise the simple; the precepts of the Lord are right, rejoicing the heart; the commandment of the Lord is pure, enlightening the eyes; the fear of the Lord is clean, enduring forever; the rules of the Lord are true, and righteous altogether. More to be desired are they than gold, even much fine gold; sweeter also than honey and drippings of the honeycomb.

Moreover, by them is your servant warned; in keeping them there is great reward." Psalm 19:7-11

3. Commit to engaging with God's word. Ask the Spirit to guide you to all that he longs to show you. Receive a greater hunger for God's teaching. Allow your desires to be stirred toward transformation by hearing and doing the word of God.

"Your words were found, and I ate them, and your words became to me a joy and the delight of my heart, for I am called by your name, O Lord, God of hosts." Jeremiah 15:16

"My son, be attentive to my words; incline your ear to my sayings. Let them not escape from your sight; keep them within your heart. For they are life to those who find them, and healing to all their flesh. Keep your heart with all vigilance, for from it flow the springs of life." Proverbs 4:20-23

We'll spend the next week being taught by the parables of Jesus, so make it your goal to receive a hunger for his word in prayer. Meditate on all that God wants to do in you through his word. Allow desire for his teaching to be stirred as you think about the abundant life he wants to lead you to through Scripture. Think of areas in which you need restoration and wisdom. And commit to engaging in the process of incredible transformation God has in store for you.

Extended Reading: Psalm 1

Forgiveness

WEEK

"As far as the east is from the west, so
far does he remove our transgressions
from us." Psalm 103:12

WEEKLY OVERVIEW

Offering forgiveness to others is one of the most difficult and important aspects of the Christian life. The Bible clearly commands us to forgive others. God longs to fashion us into his likeness that we might model the love we've been shown to a world with no concept of mercy. He longs for us to offer grace and forgiveness to the undeserving as we have been offered grace and forgiveness when we were undeserving. May you be filled with courage and boldness to offer forgiveness to those in desperate need of grace. And may God's love shine through as you enter into your calling as a minister of reconciliation.

The Nature of Forgiveness is Mercy

DAY 8

DEVOTIONAL

We would be wholly lost if it weren't for the abundant mercy of our heavenly Father. Romans 3:23-24 says, *"For all have sinned and fall short of the glory of God, and are justified by his grace as a gift, through the redemption that is in Christ Jesus."* We are offered total and complete forgiveness of our sins because God loves us and has mercy on us. The mercy of God allots us freedom and restored relationship we could never attain on our own. We are not justified by our own works or inherent worth, but by grace alone.

*"Be merciful, even as your Father is merciful.
Judge not, and you will not be judged;
condemn not, and you will not be condemned;
forgive, and you will be forgiven."*

LUKE 6:36-37

The nature of forgiveness is mercy. And the Bible tells us in Luke 6:36-37, *"Be merciful, even as your Father is merciful. Judge not, and you will not be judged; condemn not, and you will not be condemned; forgive, and you will be forgiven."* In order for us to be merciful with others, we must be consistently encountering and reflecting on the abundant mercy of God toward us. When we were at our lowest, God met us and offered us eternal, abundant life in him. When we had no ability to attain right standing before our Creator, he brought himself low, took on the form of a servant, and died for our sakes (Philippians 2:8).

You were saved by the greatest act of mercy the world will ever know. And now your heavenly Father is asking you to share the great mercy you have been shown. He's asking you to live and operate in his likeness by loving others the way you have been loved. The Bible commands us to forgive others. God doesn't give us the option. Colossians 3:13 says, *"Bearing with one another and, if one has a complaint against another, forgiving each other; as the Lord has forgiven you, so you also must forgive."* James 2:13 says, *"For judgment is without mercy to one who*

has shown no mercy. Mercy triumphs over judgment." If we are living with unforgiveness, we are living outside of the will of God.

God knows forgiveness is difficult. He knows that it takes courage and strength to offer mercy where it is undeserved. He paid the highest price for our sins by sending Jesus to an undeserving, gruesome death. But he also knows the joy that comes from reconciliation. He knows the goodness of wiping the slate clean that he might have restored relationship with us. And he longs for you to be a minister of reconciliation to all who have hurt you. He longs to overwhelm you with his love and mercy to the degree that offering others mercy and love comes from a place of overflow rather than your own strength. He longs to fill you with courage and perspective so that you can forgive those who need a glimpse of his mercy and grace.

Take time as you enter into guided prayer to receive the love and mercy of your heavenly Father. Allow him to fill you up to overflowing today. And follow his guidance as he gives you grace to forgive others in obedience and love.

47

GUIDED PRAYER

1. Meditate on the forgiveness and mercy you have been shown in Christ. Allow the compassion God has for you to fill you with compassion for others. Ask God to give you his heart for others as you meditate on his word.

"But when the goodness and loving kindness of God our Savior appeared, he saved us, not because of works done by us in righteousness, but according to his own mercy, by the washing of regeneration and renewal of the Holy Spirit, whom he poured out on us richly through Jesus Christ our Savior, so that being justified by his grace we might become heirs according to the hope of eternal life." Titus 3:4-7

"But God, being rich in mercy, because of the great love with which he loved us, even when we were dead in our trespasses, made us alive together with Christ—by grace you have been saved—and raised us up with him and seated us with him in the heavenly places in Christ Jesus, so that in the coming ages he might show the immeasurable riches of his grace in kindness toward us in Christ Jesus." Ephesians 2:4-7

2. Now meditate on God's command for you to forgive others. Make God's word the foundation of your actions rather than your own desires or fears. God will always guide you into what is absolutely best for you. You have to trust him at his word and obey.

"Be merciful, even as your Father is merciful. Judge not, and you will not be judged; condemn not, and you will not be condemned; forgive, and you will be forgiven." Luke 6:36-37

"Go and learn what this means, 'I desire mercy, and not sacrifice.' For I came not to call the righteous, but sinners." Matthew 9:13

"Bearing with one another and, if one has a complaint against another, forgiving each other; as the Lord has forgiven you, so you also must forgive." Colossians 3:13

3. Ask the Holy Spirit to reveal to you any unforgiveness in your heart. Whether the wound is large or small, you must engage in forgiveness for it to heal properly. Ask God to give you courage to forgive today.

Trusting and obeying God is foundational to experiencing the fullness of life Jesus died to give you. God longs to lead you into his perfect plans. He is always guiding and shepherding you to your best possible life. But he cannot lead you where you will not follow. He cannot bless you if you are living outside of his will. Commit to following him wherever he leads, whether or not you feel like it or understand. Allow the Holy Spirit to guide you into a lifestyle of continual forgiveness that you might experience to even greater depths the abundant life God longs to give.

Extended Reading: Luke 6

Our Forgiveness in Jesus

DEVOTIONAL

Before we have the ability to live a lifestyle of forgiveness, we must discover the depth of forgiveness we have received in Jesus. God's love is the foundation for our own love. His forgiveness is the foundation for our own forgiveness. In order to love to greater depths, we must continuously reflect on the nature of our own sin and God's overwhelming mercy.

"Be kind to one another, tenderhearted, forgiving one another, as God in Christ forgave you."

EPHESIANS 4:32

In Luke 7:44-47 Jesus reveals an important spiritual principle about forgiveness, sacrifice, and love. A sinful woman has just come and ministered to Jesus, cleaning his feet with her own tears, hair, and alabaster ointment. When Simon, a Pharisee, saw the incredible act of love, he judged the woman and Jesus in his heart. Knowing Simon's thoughts, Jesus says to him,

Do you see this woman? I entered your house; you gave me no water for my feet, but she has wet my feet with her tears and wiped them with her hair. You gave me no kiss, but from the time I came in she has not ceased to kiss my feet. You did not anoint my head with oil, but she has anointed my feet with ointment. Therefore I tell you, her sins, which are many, are forgiven—for she loved much. But he who is forgiven little, loves little.

"He who is forgiven little, loves little." Allow Jesus' words to settle into your heart for a minute. God turns our greatest sins into his greatest triumphs. He takes our greatest transgressions, offers us mercy for them all, and transforms them into life-giving rivers of love and forgiveness. Until you and I understand the depth to which we were enslaved to sin, we will never love to our greatest potential. Until we understand how vast the chasm was that separated us from

God and compare it to our new position seated with Christ in the heavenly places, we will never forgive others to the depth God calls us to.

While we were by nature wholly unworthy, God called us out from darkness and brought us into the light. While we were unable to pursue righteousness, God saved us and gave us a new identity as his sons and daughters made righteous and pure. Before the forgiveness offered you through Christ, you had no access to true relationship with your heavenly Father. You had no access to the fruit of the Spirit. You had no way to know and experience the depths of God's love. Your life was rooted in destruction with no way out. Yet God saw fit to forgive every transgression you have ever committed and will commit. The Father so longed for your restoration to him that he paid the highest price of Jesus' death.

Take time today to truly reflect on the depravity to which you once belonged and on the new nature, portion, and depth of relationship available to you by the forgiveness of God. Allow the Lord to forgive any present failures that are robbing you of the abundant life Jesus died to give you. And allow the Spirit to fill you with compassion and mercy for others that you might forgive them in response to the forgiveness you have received.

51

GUIDED PRAYER

1. Meditate on your life before salvation and your life after salvation. Allow God's word to paint a picture of just how powerful and merciful God's forgiveness is.

"Behold, the Lord's hand is not shortened, that it cannot save, or his ear dull, that it cannot hear; but your iniquities have made a separation between you and your God, and your sins have hidden his face from you so that he does not hear." Isaiah 59:1-2

"For the wages of sin is death, but the free gift of God is eternal life in Christ Jesus our Lord." Romans 6:23

"Blessed be the God and Father of our Lord Jesus Christ, who has blessed us in Christ with every spiritual blessing in the heavenly places, even as he chose us in him before the foundation of the world, that we should be holy and blameless before him." Ephesians 1:3-4

2. What sin would the Lord have you confess today? Where do you need forgiveness?

3. Ask the Holy Spirit to fill you with compassion for others today. Ask him to make you quick to forgive in light of the forgiveness you've been shown. Ask him to help you keep no record of wrongs so that you can love others with his love.

"Be kind to one another, tenderhearted, forgiving one another, as God in Christ forgave you." Ephesians 4:32

"Then Peter came up and said to him, 'Lord, how often will my brother sin against me, and I forgive him? As many as seven times?' Jesus said to him, 'I do not say to you seven times, but seventy times seven.'" Matthew 18:21-22

May Psalm 103:10-14 fill you with love for your heavenly Father and compassion for others today:

He does not deal with us according to our sins, nor repay us according to our iniquities. For as high as the heavens are above the earth, so great is his steadfast love toward those who fear him; as far as the east is from the west, so far does he remove our transgressions from us. As a father shows compassion to his children, so the Lord shows compassion to those who fear him. For he knows our frame; he remembers that we are dust.

Extended Reading: Luke 7

Healing Past Wounds and Forgiving Present Scars

DAY 10

DEVOTIONAL

All of us have experienced trial and pain. All of us are living life wounded and scarred. We learn to deal with our wounds and press forward, but whether we acknowledge it or not, wounds and scars change us. There are no perfect parents. There are no perfect friends. There are no perfect siblings or spouses. We live in an imperfect world with imperfect humans. We lash out and hurt others because we are broken and in need of healing.

"He himself bore our sins in his body on the tree,
that we might die to sin and live to righteousness.
By his wounds you have been healed."

1 PETER 2:24

One of the most critical spiritual exercises we can undergo is allowing God to heal our past wounds and guide us to a lifestyle of forgiving present scars. Without healing and forgiveness, other people's mistakes will affect our future. Without the inner working of the Holy Spirit, we will live in continual suffering from the sins of others.

Our God is a God of healing. Psalm 147:3 says, *"He heals the brokenhearted and binds up their wounds."* Psalm 103:2-4 says, *"Bless the Lord, O my soul, and forget not all his benefits, who forgives all your iniquity, who heals all your diseases, who redeems your life from the pit, who crowns you with steadfast love and mercy."* 1 Peter 2:24 says, *"He himself bore our sins in his body on the tree, that we might die to sin and live to righteousness. By his wounds you have been healed."* Your heavenly Father longs to speak to the wounded places in your life and heal them with his love.

What past experience, trial, hurtful word, or person is still harmfully affecting your life today? Where do you need the Holy Spirit to come and speak healing over you? Where do you need to cry out to God in anger or frustration over a wound? Opening the wounded places of our hearts is an emotional and difficult process, but until we allow God into the harmful events of our pasts we will never experience true freedom and restoration from them. Until we allow ourselves space to deal with what for some have been harmful and defining moments, we will never experience the entirety of the abundant life available to us.

And as the Lord begins to heal our wounds, we must allow him to guide us to a lifestyle of forgiveness for our present scars. We must forgive those people who hurt us so the scars in our lives become symbols of God's redeeming love rather than reminders of painful events. James 2:13 says, *"Mercy triumphs over judgment."* Show mercy to those who are undeserving of it just as your heavenly Father has shown you mercy. Love your enemies as Jesus did so that you can experience triumph instead of pain, freedom instead of enslavement to negativity, and joy instead of anger. May your heavenly Father be allowed to love you, hold you, and care for the places in your heart that need his healing touch the most.

55

GUIDED PRAYER

1. Meditate on God's desire to heal your wounds. Allow Scripture to fill you with courage to open your heart to the Spirit, and let him provide healing today.

"He heals the brokenhearted and binds up their wounds." Psalm 147:3

"But he was wounded for our transgressions; he was crushed for our iniquities; upon him was the chastisement that brought us peace, and with his stripes we are healed." Isaiah 53:5

"Come to me, all who labor and are heavy laden, and I will give you rest." Matthew 11:28

2. Ask the Holy Spirit to show you what he wants to heal today. What wound is affecting your life? Where do you need God to speak his truth and love over you?

3. Open your heart to the Lord and ask him to speak truth and love to your wound. Ask the Holy Spirit to heal your wounds in whatever way he desires. Trust and follow his leadership.

"The Lord your God is in your midst, a mighty one who will save; he will rejoice over you with gladness; he will quiet you by his love; he will exult over you with loud singing." Zephaniah 3:17

"Bless the Lord, O my soul, and forget not all his benefits, who forgives all your iniquity, who heals all your diseases, who redeems your life from the pit, who crowns you with steadfast love and mercy." Psalm 103:2-4

Receiving healing for wounds and the courage to forgive present scars is a constant process. There will always be more for the Lord to heal. There will always be new wounds the Lord wants to speak to. If you will allow the Lord to faithfully love and heal your wounds, you will experience abundant life to greater depths than you thought possible. May you be filled with newfound courage and freedom today in response to the overwhelming love and power of your heavenly Father.

Extended Reading: Psalm 147

A Lifestyle of Continual Forgiveness

DAY 11

DEVOTIONAL

Ephesians 4:26-27 offers revelation on an important and often unknown spiritual principle. Scripture says, *"Be angry and do not sin; do not let the sun go down on your anger, and give no opportunity to the devil."* When we allow anger to fester within us for days, weeks, months, and sometimes years, we allow the enemy to gain a foothold in our lives that robs us of the

*"Be angry and do not sin; do not let the sun go down
on your anger, and give no opportunity to the devil."*

EPHESIANS 4:26-27

abundant life provided in Christ. In Ephesians, Paul is clear that anger in itself is not a sin; it's when we allow anger to remain instead of choosing grace and forgiveness that we break God's command.

When people wrong us the natural response is to be angry, and that is all right! Jesus himself was often angry. Matthew 21:12 tells us, *"And Jesus entered the temple and drove out all who sold and bought in the temple, and he overturned the tables of the money-changers and the seats of those who sold pigeons."* Jesus was consistently angry with those who claimed to know God and took advantage of others. Nothing made him more angry than pharisaical people. But Jesus also modeled forgiveness of the highest form. Rather than being filled with anger and allowing it to fester inside of him, he offered his life out of his love for the very people who shouted, *"Crucify him!"* and *"Free Barabbas!"*

The truth is that our anger is often a symptom of our brokenness rather than the result of the wrongs of others. Often, anger is rooted in our own insecurities and pride rather than a righteous anger for justice. It's for this reason the Bible tells us over and over again to be slow to anger. James 1:19-20 says, *"Know this, my beloved brothers: let every person be quick to hear, slow to speak, slow to anger; for the anger of man does not produce the righteousness of God."* Proverbs 19:11 says, *"Good sense makes one slow to anger, and it is his glory to overlook an offense."* And Proverbs 29:11 says, *"A fool gives full vent to his spirit, but a wise man quietly holds it back."*

The Lord desires to make us a people filled with his grace and compassion over our own anger and prideful sense of justice. God, who was deserving of everything, gave it all up to show us grace. Jesus is the rightful King of kings and Lord of lords. But rather than claiming what was rightfully his own, he humbled himself before a Roman prefect and a rebellious people and gave up his own life. And now he asks you to do the same. Jesus is asking you to lay down your rights and pride to pursue a higher calling of unconditional love. He's asking you to show grace where none is deserved. He's asking you to offer mercy where there should rightfully be none. And he's asking you to forgive others so that heaven might come to earth through your actions. Commit to living a lifestyle of continual forgiveness today, and allow God to work through you to bring salvation and restored relationship to a world in desperate need of a Savior.

GUIDED PRAYER

1. Meditate on God's command to live a lifestyle of continual forgiveness. Allow his word to fill you with a desire to be slow to anger and quick to forgive and offer grace.

"Be angry and do not sin; do not let the sun go down on your anger, and give no opportunity to the devil." Ephesians 4:26-27

"Whoever is slow to anger is better than the mighty, and he who rules his spirit than he who takes a city." Proverbs 16:32

"Be kind to one another, tenderhearted, forgiving one another, as God in Christ forgave you." Ephesians 4:32

2. Who do you need to offer forgiveness to today? What anger have you allowed to fester in your heart?

3. Forgive that person or those people in your heart right now. Offer grace to them in your heart that you might receive healing in the place of bitterness.

"Know this, my beloved brothers: let every person be quick to hear, slow to speak, slow to anger; for the anger of man does not produce the righteousness of God." James 1:19-20

"And whenever you stand praying, forgive, if you have anything against anyone, so that your Father also who is in heaven may forgive you your trespasses." Mark 11:25

1 Peter 2:23 says, *"When he was reviled, he did not revile in return; when he suffered, he did not threaten, but continued entrusting himself to him who judges justly."* May we become like Jesus and offer grace and forgiveness to others who are undeserving. May we be reflections of his love by being slow to anger and quick to offer mercy. May his light shine through us today into a world wrought with darkness and pain.

Extended Reading: Ephesians 4

Forgive the Person, Not Their Actions

DEVOTIONAL

One of the most important distinctions to make when learning about the practice of forgiveness is to forgive the person, not their actions. Playing the sequence of someone's wrongful action over and over again in the mind is a terrible hindrance to obeying God's command to forgive. When we continually reflect on how wrong an action was, our thoughts act as a blockade between our hearts and God's heavenly compassion.

"A new commandment I give to you, that you love one another: just as I have loved you, you also are to love one another."

John 13:34 tells us, *"A new commandment I give to you, that you love one another: just as I have loved you, you also are to love one another."* God forgives us because he loves us, not because our actions are ever worthy of forgiveness. He forgives us because he values restored relationship with us over our sins. He forgives us because he is filled with love for us, not because our acts of confession demand forgiveness from him. And he says, *"Just as I have loved you, you also are to love one another."* When Peter denied Jesus three times, he offered him relationship and another opportunity to serve him. When Thomas was filled with doubt, Jesus offered him his nail-pierced hands. And when we sin against God, he offers us forgiveness that we might receive the full depths of his love again.

Luke 6:37 says, *"Judge not, and you will not be judged; condemn not, and you will not be condemned; forgive, and you will be forgiven."* Our job is not to judge or condemn the actions of another. The only one worthy of passing judgment is already seated on his throne. God alone is perfect and able to offer sound judgment.

He alone carries the burden of being King of kings and Lord of lords. And he continually chooses to show mercy and compassion on the undeserving. He continually offers forgiveness to the unworthy and sinful. He continually runs out to meet us in our sin, like the father of the prodigal son.

Showing compassion for the wrongful actions of another is not easy, but it is necessary. If we are to live a lifestyle of continual forgiveness the way God commands, we must look to heart of the person and receive God's compassion rather than taking up the seat of judgement. If we are to love one another as God has loved us, we must value relationship over worldly justice and give grace where none is deserved. May we obtain access to the heart of our heavenly Father today as we seek to love as he loves. May we be filled with compassion for others after reflection on the overwhelming grace we've been shown. And may we be filled with courage and strength to reach past a wrongful action and forgive the person from our hearts.

GUIDED PRAYER

1. Meditate on God's command to *"judge not."* Allow Scripture to renew your mind to the important command to forgive others.

"Judge not, and you will not be judged; condemn not, and you will not be condemned; forgive, and you will be forgiven." Luke 6:37

"Whoever covers an offense seeks love, but he who repeats a matter separates close friends." Proverbs 17:9

2. What action has been deemed unforgivable in your mind? Where are you struggling to forgive a person because of the way they've wronged you?

3. Ask God to give you the ability to look past a wrongful action to the heart of the person so that you might have compassion and offer forgiveness. Spend time in his presence removing yourself from the seat of judgment so that you can offer grace and forgiveness.

"He does not deal with us according to our sins, nor repay us according to our iniquities. For as high as the heavens are above the earth, so great is his steadfast love toward those who fear him; as far as the east is from the west, so far does he remove our transgressions from us. As a father shows compassion to his children, so the Lord shows compassion to those who fear him. For he knows our frame; he remembers that we are dust." Psalm 103:10-14

When we offer forgiveness where none is deserved, we are placing our hope for justice and reconciliation in God rather than ourselves. When we offer mercy we look to heaven for all things to be set right and renewed rather than looking to this fallen and folly-filled world. There is no perfection in this world. There is nothing we can do to completely rid this world of its inherent depravity. So we must look to our heavenly Father to work and heal as he wills and follow in his footsteps. We must carry an atmosphere of grace so that heaven can meet earth through our lives and draw people into the fold of God. May we have the strength and perspective to place our hope in heaven and offer mercy, compassion, and forgiveness to the wrongful, destitute, and proud.

Extended Reading: John 13

Living Without Expectation of Perfection

DEVOTIONAL

One of the most vital aspects of offering continual forgiveness is living without expectation of perfection from others. You will never meet a perfect human. All of us suffer from the same sinful, broken condition. And as believers, our lives are a reflection of God's grace transforming what was once wholly sinful into

*"For all have sinned and fall
short of the glory of God."*

ROMANS 3:23

pictures of his love. Even in this reflection, we will never experience perfection until we pass from this world to the next and live in perfect, uninhibited relationship with our heavenly Father.

Psalm 103:10-14 offers us insight into the expectations of God in regards to our sin. May the perspective of our heavenly Father be our model for forgiveness:

He does not deal with us according to our sins, nor repay us according to our iniquities. For as high as the heavens are above the earth, so great is his steadfast love toward those who fear him; as far as the east is from the west, so far does he remove our transgressions from us. As a father shows compassion to his children, so the Lord shows compassion to those who fear him. For he knows our frame; he remembers that we are dust.

God offers us continual love, grace, compassion, and forgiveness because he knows that we've come from dust and will return to dust once again. He knows the sins and symptoms of brokenness that entangle us. And he offers us forgiveness for our sin and grace to live righteously in the future. If we are ever going to live in the fullness of life available to us, we must learn to be like our Father. We must learn

to live without an expectation of perfection from anyone. It isn't pessimistic to view everyone as imperfect. Rather, it's a perspective that will allow us to love and enjoy others to the fullest.

Our heavenly Father longs to guide us to a lifestyle of forgiveness because he longs for us to live with the fullness of joy. Our God's greatest delight is relationship with his people, and it was in forgiveness by the death of Jesus that restored relationship was made possible. We are made in the image of our Father. We are created to enjoy fellowship with one another, uninhibited by the bitterness and resentment that comes from unforgiveness. We are made to have our hearts open and full of love for one another. But in order to live the abundant life, we must free ourselves from placing others on a platform of perfection they will never attain.

Take time in guided prayer to allow God to fill you with his perspective. Allow him to set you free from the expectation of perfection for others. Romans 3:23 says, *"For all have sinned and fall short of the glory of God."* May you become like your heavenly Father: filled with love, grace, and forgiveness for all those who fall short of perfection around you.

GUIDED PRAYER

1. Meditate on the nature of our imperfection as humans. Allow God's word to fill you with grace for the sins and mistakes of others.

"Surely there is not a righteous man on earth who does good and never sins." Ecclesiastes 7:20

"For all have sinned and fall short of the glory of God." Romans 3:23

2. Who have you been elevating to the status of perfection? Whom do you need to offer grace to who didn't meet your expectations?

3. Ask the Lord to fill you with grace, mercy, and forgiveness for others. Ask him to give you his perspective. Allow the Holy Spirit to lead you to a greater portion of joy and life today as you free others from the expectation of perfection.

"He does not deal with us according to our sins, nor repay us according to our iniquities. For as high as the heavens are above the earth, so great is his steadfast love toward those who fear him; as far as the east is from the west, so far does he remove our transgressions from us. As a father shows compassion to his children, so the Lord shows compassion to those who fear him. For he knows our frame; he remembers that we are dust." Psalm 103:10-14

Along with freeing others from the expectation of perfection, if we will offer ourselves the same grace and mercy that our heavenly Father does, we will experience new levels of joy and freedom. While God has offered us a path to total freedom from sin, he has the fullness of compassion for our weaknesses. Don't strive for perfection in your works, but instead pursue a deeper relationship with the God of love and grace. You weren't created to live perfectly in your own strength, but to know the love of the Father and allow him to empower you for the life to which you have been called. May you free yourself from the burden of perfection today and pursue greater intimacy with your heavenly Father.

Extended Reading: Psalm 103

Forgiving Yourself

DEVOTIONAL

As Christians striving to love others well and live in obedience to the commands of Christ, we often are harder on ourselves than our heavenly Father is. If we are ever going to experience the depths of God's love in every season, we must learn to forgive ourselves. In Brennan Manning's book, *Abba's Child: The Cry of the Heart for Intimate Belonging*, he writes a powerful

*"Whoever conceals his transgressions will not prosper, but
he who confesses and forsakes them will obtain mercy."*

PROVERBS 28:13

statement that has the ability to both guide us to a greater lifestyle of peace and open the door of our hearts to greater affections from our heavenly Father:

"But we cannot assume that He feels about us the way we feel about ourselves—unless we love ourselves compassionately, intensely, and freely. In human form Jesus revealed to us what God is like. He exposed our projections for the idolatry that they are and gave us the way to become free of them. It takes a profound conversion to accept that God is relentlessly tender and compassionate toward us just as we are—not in spite of our sins and faults (that would not be total acceptance), but with them. Though God does not condone or sanction evil, He does not withhold his love because there is evil in us."

Our Father loves us unconditionally. His grace and mercy will never run out. He is never surprised when we sin or fall short of the life to which we've been called because he knows our need of him. He knows that without his help we will never succeed in living a lifestyle of obedience. He knows that without consistent encounters with his love we will never be able to fully love others. And he knows that without being consistently filled with the Holy Spirit we will never be empowered to live in the freedom from sin Christ's death affords us.

1 John 2:1 says, *"My little children, I am writing these things to you so that you may not sin. But if anyone does sin, we have an advocate with the Father, Jesus Christ the righteous."* God does not condone our sin. He does not enjoy our mistakes. But he will meet us in our place of brokenness and need every time we fail. He will offer us mercy and compassion every time we come to him in confession and repentance. And nothing could ever cause him to stop loving us for even a moment.

Your heavenly Father is beckoning you to forgive yourself today. He's waiting to fill you with his mercy and grace to overflowing. He's ready to lead you into a lifestyle of loving yourself as he has loved you. Run out to meet him today. Allow him to clothe you with love, honor, and grace. Allow him to show you the depths of his compassion for you. And live today in light of the glorious grace of Jesus.

71

GUIDED PRAYER

1. Meditate on the importance of forgiving yourself. Allow Scripture to give you God's perspective of grace and mercy.

"But he was pierced for our transgressions; he was crushed for our iniquities; upon him was the chastisement that brought us peace, and with his wounds we are healed."
Isaiah 53:5

"I do not nullify the grace of God, for if righteousness were through the law, then Christ died for no purpose."
Galatians 2:21

"For all have sinned and fall short of the glory of God."
Romans 3:23

2. Where do you need to forgive yourself today?
What mistake or failure are you carrying around like a weight? Where are you not offering yourself the grace and mercy offered by your heavenly Father?

3. Ask God to share with you his perspective.
Ask him to help you see yourself as he sees you.

Spend time resting in his love and compassion and being filled with his affections to overflowing.

"No, in all these things we are more than conquerors through him who loved us. For I am sure that neither death nor life, nor angels nor rulers, nor things present nor things to come, nor powers, nor height nor depth, nor anything else in all creation, will be able to separate us from the love of God in Christ Jesus our Lord."
Romans 8:37-39

Often we carry the weight of our mistakes because we are unwilling to ask forgiveness from others. Confessing and repenting to those we've wronged is a vital part of the Christian life. Admitting our weaknesses and faults to others helps remove us from the pursuit of perfection and guide us to a life of surrender and humility. Confess your sins and ask for forgiveness from anyone you've wronged. And allow the forgiveness of your heavenly Father to fill you with joy, love, and freedom where only sin and shame abounded before.

Extended Reading: Romans 8

Prodigal son

WEEK

"'For this my son was dead, and is alive again; he was lost, and is found.'" Luke 15:24

WEEKLY OVERVIEW

The story of the prodigal son moves my heart to delve into the depths of God's limitless grace. I find myself in every facet of Jesus' words. I identify with both the son's rebellion and the power of the father's love. As children of God we are in constant need of reminders about God's mercy toward us. When the world rejects us, God calls us in. When the world writes us off, God clothes us with righteousness and honor. May this transformative story of the prodigal son guide you to a deeper and more intimate relationship with your loving heavenly Father.

God Demonstrates His Grace

DAY 15

DEVOTIONAL

No single passage of Scripture has impacted my life in greater ways than Jesus' parable of the prodigal son. I find myself in every facet of this story. I see my own sin and pride in the foolishness of the son to run from the Father. I see the despair and destitution that results from my own sin as the son longs for the slop he feeds to pigs. I see my desperate need for forgiveness, grace, and restoration in the son's return. And more than anything, I see the unfathomable grace of my heavenly Father as the father in the story runs out to embrace his disobedient and wayward child.

Rather than beginning this week on the prodigal son with my own thoughts, take time to allow the entirety of Jesus' words in this transformative story to impact your life. Ask the Holy Spirit for fresh eyes today. Find yourself in Jesus' words. I pray that you will feel the selfishness and rebellion in the prodigal son. I pray that you will feel the despair and loneliness that comes from sin and separation from the Father. And I pray that you will feel the loving embrace of your heavenly Father as the heart of your God is clearly displayed through this life-changing story.

"There was a man who had two sons. And the younger of them said to his father, 'Father, give me the share of property that is coming to me.' And he divided his property between them. Not many days later, the younger son gathered all he had and took a journey into a far country, and there he squandered his property in reckless living. And when he had spent everything, a severe famine arose in that country, and he began to be in need. So he went and hired himself out to one of the citizens of that country, who sent him into his fields to feed pigs. And he was longing to be fed with the pods that the pigs ate, and no one gave him anything.

*"And from his fullness we have all
received, grace upon grace."*

JOHN 1:6

"But when he came to himself, he said, 'How many of my father's hired servants have more than enough bread, but I perish here with hunger! I will arise and go to my father, and I will say to him, "Father, I have sinned against heaven and before you. I am no longer worthy to be called your son. Treat me as one of your hired servants."' And he arose and came to his father. But while he was still a long way off, his father saw him and felt compassion, and ran and embraced him and kissed him. And the son said to him, 'Father, I have sinned against heaven and before you. I am no longer worthy to be called your son.' But the father said to his servants, 'Bring quickly the best robe, and put it on him, and put a ring on his hand, and shoes on his feet. And bring the fattened calf and kill it, and let us eat and celebrate. For this my son was dead, and is alive again; he was lost, and is found.' And they began to celebrate.

"Now his older son was in the field, and as he came and drew near to the house, he heard music and dancing. And he called one of the servants and asked what these things meant. And he said to him, 'Your brother has come, and your father has killed the fattened calf, because he has received him back safe and sound.' But he was angry and refused to go in. His father came out and entreated him, but he answered his father, 'Look, these many years I have served you, and I never disobeyed your command, yet you never gave me a young goat, that I might celebrate with my friends. But when this son of yours came, who has devoured your property with prostitutes, you killed the fattened calf for him!' And he said to him, 'Son, you are always with me, and all that is mine is yours. It was fitting to celebrate and be glad, for this your brother was dead, and is alive; he was lost, and is found'" (Luke 15:11-32).

GUIDED PRAYER

1. Place yourself in every facet of the story. Find your own story of redemption and reconciliation in Jesus' words.

2. Where do you need the grace of your heavenly Father today? What part of your life needs the redeeming love of God?

3. Turn to the Father and confess your sin. Confess your need of his embrace and forgiveness. Allow him to forgive and heal the areas of your life wrought with the destruction of sin.

We are in constant need of God's grace. We will never live a perfect day. We will never step outside an immense need to be unconditionally loved and forgiven by our Father. Sin robs us of the abundant life available to us in Jesus every day. And until we allow God to forgive and heal the sinful places in our lives we will not experience the tremendous power and grace of our heavenly Father in those areas. May you spend the entirety of your day wrapped up in the arms of your Father. May he speak a new identity over you as his child both forgiven and empowered for freedom. And may you experience the abundant life only found in receiving the overwhelming and free grace of God.

Extended Reading: John 1

DEVOTIONAL

Our heavenly Father is abundantly patient with us. So vast is his love that our hearts can always be filled with his affection. So perfect is his leadership and wisdom that he makes available to us a perfect and pleasing life through every season. And yet he is patient to guide us into the fullness of life afforded to us by Christ's sacrifice. He waits, sweetly beckoning us to simply trust him and cultivate a heart of constant communion with him.

*"But you, O Lord, are a God merciful
and gracious, slow to anger and abounding
in steadfast love and faithfulness."*

PSALM 86:15

In Luke 15, Jesus tells us of a prodigal son who foolishly and pridefully leaves perfect communion with his father to chase after worldly satisfaction. The father lovingly obliges his son, offers him his inheritance as if he himself were dead, and watches as his son leaves a life in his father's care to lead a lifestyle of destruction. And the father waits, patiently hoping for the return of his child.

I find myself daily leaving the perfection of communion with my heavenly Father to seek the things of the world. I seek after success and admiration from the lost and broken rather than simply receiving the unconditional acceptance of my Father. I abandon perfect peace for the striving and stress of worldly gain. I reject the loving and perfect thoughts of my Father for the fleeting and unfounded affection of others.

I am the prodigal son. We all are. And yet our heavenly Father has a patient heart toward us. He waits to run out to meet us. Psalm 86:15 says, *"But you, O Lord, are a God merciful and gracious, slow to anger and abounding in steadfast love and faithfulness."* Just when I think my heavenly Father will reject me for my sin and rebellion, he runs out to clothe me with the best robe, a ring, and new shoes (Luke 15:22). Just when I think he'll send me off to the fields as a slave for punishment, he throws a feast in my honor (Luke 15:23-24). Just when I think I am unworthy of his affections and attention, he reminds me of the death of his Son, sacrificed that I might receive the abundance of unconditional love and grace my Father has toward me.

I long to live in the embrace of my Father. I long to end my days of wayward pursuits. I long to rest in the perfect communion available to me in Jesus. There is no source of true love apart from him. There is no relationship more satisfying than one with our God. There is no identity more freeing than being the child of the Creator. And there is no real grace outside of his overwhelmingly patient heart.

May we, as the bride of Christ, turn our feet toward the home of our Father and confess our need of him. May we humble ourselves before a God who is both patient and powerful. And may we allow him to pick us up off our knees, clothe us with honor and love, and wrap us up in his grace-filled arms. Your God is patient toward you, waiting with expectation in his heart for what he can do in your life. Receive the love he longs to give and experience the abundant life that comes only through restored relationship with your patient Father.

GUIDED PRAYER

1. Meditate on the patient heart of God. Allow his patience to draw you into the deeper places of his heart. Receive his presence and rest in the knowledge of his love.

"The Lord is not slow to fulfill his promise as some count slowness, but is patient toward you, not wishing that any should perish, but that all should reach repentance." 2 Peter 3:9

"But you, O Lord, are a God merciful and gracious, slow to anger and abounding in steadfast love and faithfulness." Psalm 86:15

"But for me it is good to be near God; I have made the Lord God my refuge, that I may tell of all your works." Psalm 73:28

2. In what ways have you been living like the prodigal son? Where have you gone your own way and abandoned the perfect peace that comes from total communion with the Father?

"You keep him in perfect peace whose mind is stayed on you, because he trusts in you." Isaiah 26:3

3. Turn your heart toward the Father, repent of your sin, and allow him to fill you with his abundant love. Ask him to reveal his love to you today right where you're at. Ask him how he feels about you. And let his love wash away any shame or guilt that would keep you from experiencing the full breadth of his affection.

"I sought the Lord, and he answered me and delivered me from all my fears. Those who look to him are radiant, and their faces shall never be ashamed." Psalm 34:4-5

The patience of our Father is by no means a weakness as the world might think. Our God is patient because he has perfect perspective and purpose. He values that which actually matters and doesn't concern himself with worldly pursuits. He sees the full path of your life. He knows the reasons for which you were created. He knows the highs and lows you will go through. And he is patient toward you. Rest in his patience. Allow his perspectives to become yours. And live today at the pace at which he guides you, trusting that his patient heart will lead you to his perfect and pleasing will.

Extended Reading: 2 Peter 3

DEVOTIONAL

One of the most powerful verses in Scripture is found in Luke 15:20. Take a minute this morning to reflect on the forgiving heart of your heavenly Father as you read this Scripture: *"And he arose and came to his father. But while he was still a long way off, his father saw him and felt compassion, and ran and embraced him and kissed him."*

"And he arose and came to his father. But while he was still a long way off, his father saw him and felt compassion, and ran and embraced him and kissed him."

LUKE 15:20

Our heavenly Father is quick to forgive us no matter how great our sin. He longs for us to turn our hearts toward him so that he can run out to meet us in our brokenness and weakness and draw us back into total communion with him. Too often we wait to turn our hearts toward the Father. Too often we allow the lack of grace in others to instill in us a belief that God will be mad and slow to forgive us if we confess to him.

The truth is that God is constantly aware of our sin, and yet he longs for intimacy with us in every moment. You are never too dirty to be wrapped up in the loving arms of your Father. You are never too broken to be clothed with his righteousness and honor. You never step outside of being his fully loved and forgiven child. If you will turn your heart toward him the instant you sin, you will discover a continual wellspring of grace and love that never runs dry and never holds back. God is filled with grace and love for you all the time no matter how great the sin or how long it has been since you've turned your heart toward him.

1 John 1:9 says, *"If we confess our sins, he is faithful and just to forgive us our sins and to cleanse us from all unrighteousness."* The moment you confess, you are brought back into total freedom and righteousness. The forgiveness of God cleanses you through and through. There is always joy, peace, purpose, and hope on the other side of confession. There is always intimate, restored relationship available to you. All that is required of you is to open your heart to the Father in faith that he will always love you and receive the overwhelming love he longs to give you.

What area of your heart has yet to receive the fullness of God's love? Where do you need his instant forgiveness? What are you hiding from the Father in fear of how he will react to your sin? Place yourself in the prodigal son story today. Open your heart to the Father in a posture of repentance and set your feet toward him. Go to him and confess your sins, weaknesses, and need of him. Picture yourself at the feet of the Father who has run out to meet you, and receive all the love and restoration he has to give you today. There is nothing more important than allowing yourself to be fully available to your heavenly Father and taking time to be fully loved by him. May you have a transformational encounter with your Father today as you enter into guided prayer.

GUIDED PRAYER

1. Meditate on the importance of having your heart fully available to the Lord. Reflect on the importance of confession.

"Keep your heart with all vigilance, for from it flow the springs of life." Proverbs 4:23

"Trust in the Lord with all your heart, and do not lean on your own understanding. In all your ways acknowledge him, and he will make straight your paths." Proverbs 3:5-6

"Whoever conceals his transgressions will not prosper, but he who confesses and forsakes them will obtain mercy." Proverbs 28:13

2. Confess any sin you have and acknowledge your need of God's love and forgiveness. Picture yourself at the feet of the Father as he runs out to meet you, and make your heart fully available to him.

"Repent therefore, and turn again, that your sins may be blotted out." Acts 3:19

3. Receive the love and forgiveness of your heavenly Father. Ask him to show you how he feels about you. Ask him to help you experience the cleansing power of his forgiveness. Take time to rest in his love and allow it to transform you.

"If we confess our sins, he is faithful and just to forgive us our sins and to cleanse us from all unrighteousness." 1 John 1:9

While God certainly knows everything about our hearts, he waits to transform, renew, and fill them until we open them up to receive. He is not a God that forces what we need but waits for us patiently and expectantly. As children of such a loving God, it's vital that we cultivate a posture of need and receptiveness. It's vital that we till the soil of our hearts to fully receive God's love and bear the fruit of his presence in our lives. Take time throughout your day to check the posture of your heart and open any areas that are closed off. Allow him to guide you in every way. Trust him and live in obedience. May you live today in total communion with your heavenly Father.

Extended Reading: 1 John 1

# of Sonship

DEVOTIONAL

By the sacrifice of Jesus, you and I have been made sons and daughters of the Most High God. We've been redeemed and transformed into children and heirs to the kingdom of God. Romans 8:15-17 says,

*"And I will be a father to you, and you shall be sons
and daughters to me, says the Lord Almighty."*

2 CORINTHIANS 6:18

*For you did not receive the spirit of slavery to fall back
into fear, but you have received the Spirit of adoption
as sons, by whom we cry, "Abba! Father!" The Spirit
himself bears witness with our spirit that we are children
of God, and if children, then heirs—heirs of God and
fellow heirs with Christ, provided we suffer with him in
order that we may also be glorified with him.*

In the story of the prodigal son, the father clothes his wayward and rebellious son with a robe, a ring, and sandals. All three of these symbols represent a restoration of sonship in different ways. The son who returned to his father to simply be employed as a slave was immediately restored as a child and heir. The father had no desire to make his son pay for his own sins; he simply wanted restored relationship with his child again.

Our heavenly Father feels the same way about us. At salvation we were restored to right standing in the eyes of God. 2 Corinthians 6:18 says, *"And I will be a father to you, and you shall be sons and daughters to me, says the Lord Almighty."* 1 John 3:1 says, *"See what kind of love the Father has given to us, that we should be called children of God; and so we are."* No matter what sins we commit, we will always be a child of God. No sin we ever commit can rob us from the inheritance of glorious relationship afforded to us by the death of Christ Jesus. His love is stronger than our sin.

An epidemic exists in the church today of believers living and serving their Father as slaves rather than as sons and daughters. A slave works and serves apart from intimate relationship with their master. A son lives with the empowerment of true relationship with the Father. Many disciples are trying to live for Jesus—they go to church, go on a mission trip, teach a small group, and even try and read their Bibles—but they have no real fellowship or relationship with the Father. I lived much of my Christian life that way. It wasn't until I began to experience the Father's heart (knowing that he longed for me to truly know him), experience his love and nearness, and be empowered by a new identity that I began living as a son.

Allow your heavenly Father to clothe you with his presence and speak to your true identity today. Ask him what it looks like to live as a son or daughter who truly knows the Father. And experience the overwhelming joy and peace that comes from intimate relationship with your God.

GUIDED PRAYER

1. Meditate on your identity as a son or daughter of the Most High God. Allow Scripture to fill your heart with a fresh desire to pursue deeper levels of relationship with your Father.

"And I will be a father to you, and you shall be sons and daughters to me, says the Lord Almighty." 2 Corinthians 6:18

"See what kind of love the Father has given to us, that we should be called children of God; and so we are. The reason why the world does not know us is that it did not know him." 1 John 3:1

"For you did not receive the spirit of slavery to fall back into fear, but you have received the Spirit of adoption as sons, by whom we cry, 'Abba! Father!' The Spirit himself bears witness with our spirit that we are children of God, and if children, then heirs—heirs of God and fellow heirs with Christ, provided we suffer with him in order that we may also be glorified with him." Romans 8:15-17

2. In what ways do you feel you might be living as a slave more than a son or daughter? Where are you lacking a revelation and experience of God's love for you?

3. Ask your heavenly Father to reveal the depths of his love today. Ask him to guide you into a fresh encounter with his grace. Ask him to restore you and lead you into greater depths of relationship with him.

"No, in all these things we are more than conquerors through him who loved us. For I am sure that neither death nor life, nor angels nor rulers, nor things present nor things to come, nor powers, nor height nor depth, nor anything else in all creation, will be able to separate us from the love of God in Christ Jesus our Lord." Romans 8:37-39

95

How astounding is the love and grace of our Father that we would be considered his children. How vast is his love for us that with no effort of our own we would be transformed into heirs with Christ. There is no greater privilege than being the son or daughter of the Creator. There is no greater love than that which the Father has for us. And there is no greater life than one spent in full relationship with the very Father who would run out to meet us, call us his son or daughter in our weakest moments, and bring us into his family.

Extended Reading: Romans 8

DEVOTIONAL

The restoration of identity to the rebellious and wayward son in the story of the prodigal son is perhaps the greatest example of God's heart to restore you and me as his children. In the story, the rebellious son returns to the Father hoping solely to be allowed to serve his father as one of the slaves. But as the son approached his home, the father ran out to meet him and immediately brought restoration to his identity as a good and pleasing son in his eyes.

"But you are a chosen race, a royal priesthood, a holy nation, a people for his own possession, that you may proclaim the excellencies of him who called you out of darkness into his marvelous light."

1 PETER 2:9

2 Corinthians 5:17 says, *"Therefore, if anyone is in Christ, he is a new creation. The old has passed away; behold, the new has come."* Through faith in the life, death, and resurrection of Jesus, we have been transformed from a rebellious and sinful people into reflections of our Savior. God ran out to meet us at our point of greatest weakness and clothed us with a new nature that we might no longer sin against him but live with him in glorious, powerful communion.

Isaiah 43:1 says, *"Fear not, for I have redeemed you; I have called you by name, you are mine."* Our Father saved us from a life of wandering and searching for who we are and has called us his holy and redeemed children. Our name is no longer associated with a sinful nature but rather with the bloodline of Christ Jesus. By no power of our own, we have been transformed, set free, redeemed, and made to be like our heavenly Father in both our nature and our deeds.

1 Peter 2:9 says, *"But you are a chosen race, a royal priesthood, a holy nation, a people for his own possession, that you may proclaim the excellencies of him who called*

you out of darkness into his marvelous light." We have an identity that reaches far beyond simply getting through this life happily and successfully. Our identity now is to proclaim the unimaginable excellencies of our heavenly Father. We're called to declare to the world the incredible power of our God, that he could take our weak and helpless lives, give us new names, place his Spirit within us, and ignite a passion so deep no circumstance could ever change it. This world is not your home. The nation in which you live is no longer your highest allegiance. You are the child of the Creator, the one true God, and he has made you new, whole, and purposed for works of eternal significance.

Allow your Father to declare to you your identity in Christ. Take time today to listen and receive a fresh revelation of who you are. Allow the Spirit to fill you afresh and empower you to live a life worthy of the one who has saved you. There is no greater joy than living in light of the incredible gift of a restored identity we've been given by the grace of our heavenly Father.

GUIDED PRAYER

1. Meditate on the restoration of the son's identity in the story of the prodigal son. Allow Scripture to give you perspective on your own identity in Christ.

"And the son said to him, 'Father, I have sinned against heaven and before you. I am no longer worthy to be called your son.' But the father said to his servants, 'Bring quickly the best robe, and put it on him, and put a ring on his hand, and shoes on his feet. And bring the fattened calf and kill it, and let us eat and celebrate. For this my son was dead, and is alive again; he was lost, and is found.' And they began to celebrate." Luke 15:21-24

"Therefore, if anyone is in Christ, he is a new creation. The old has passed away; behold, the new has come." 2 Corinthians 5:17

2. Ask the Holy Spirit to fill you afresh today. Take time to rest in God's presence and allow him to reveal his love for you anew.

"And do not get drunk with wine, for that is debauchery, but be filled with the Spirit." Ephesians 5:18

3. Ask the Father to show you the good works he has set before you today. Ask him to lead you into a lifestyle of proclaiming his excellencies. Ask him to empower you to live out your new identity in Christ.

"But you are a chosen race, a royal priesthood, a holy nation, a people for his own possession, that you may proclaim the excellencies of him who called you out of darkness into his marvelous light." 1 Peter 2:9

"But now thus says the Lord, he who created you, O Jacob, he who formed you, O Israel: "Fear not, for I have redeemed you; I have called you by name, you are mine." Isaiah 43:1

May Colossians 3:1-4 serve as a foundation on which we pursue the fullness of life afforded to us by the love and grace of our heavenly Father:

If then you have been raised with Christ, seek the things that are above, where Christ is, seated at the right hand of God. Set your minds on things that are above, not on things that are on earth. For you have died, and your life is hidden with Christ in God. When Christ who is your life appears, then you also will appear with him in glory.

Extended Reading: Colossians 3

# of Authority

DEVOTIONAL

One day as I spent time with the Lord I felt him speak to me, "Come follow me and I'll give you the keys to the kingdom." I stood still in awe and wonder at a God who would break through the natural and speak straight to my heart. At this point I had yet to read a Scripture that I believe was meant to define the lives of all believers. Once I came across this verse I felt the purpose for my life was changed forever.

In Matthew 16:19 Jesus tells Peter, *"I will give you the keys of the kingdom of heaven, and whatever you bind on earth shall be bound in heaven, and whatever you loose on earth shall be loosed in heaven."* And later in Matthew 18:18 he tells the rest of the disciples, *"Truly, I say to you, whatever you bind on earth shall be bound in heaven,*

and whatever you loose on earth shall be loosed in heaven." You and I are called to live with the authority of our Savior. When we became Christians we were brought into a restoration of authority only available to those transformed by his powerful sacrifice. We have been given dominion over the powers of darkness that we might spread the truth of God's authority over the works of the enemy. God has chosen to use us as beacons of his holy light that the world would see us and know of the power and love of our heavenly Father.

In the story of the prodigal son, the father immediately restores the authority of his child upon his return. When the father gives his ring to his son, we see a symbol of authority being transferred back to the son. No matter how terrible the sin, no matter how long the rebellion, our Father will always give us authority to do his work when we return to him.

No sin disqualifies us from living a life of eternal impact. No length of time outside of the church, the Bible, prayer, or worship keeps us from being ministers of God's grace. In his grace, he's chosen to use us. Each one of us has been appointed, not by our own merit, but by his love and divine wisdom to live a life of eternal significance only we can live.

Jesus is saying to you today, "Come follow me and I'll give you the keys to my kingdom." He's given you authority to bind and loose things on heaven and earth. You have the authority to lead others to freedom from the terrible schemes of the enemy on their lives. You have the ability to love and minister to others by the Spirit of God. You can shine the light of God's love into the darkest places and claim what was the enemy's for the one true God.

Take time in guided prayer to meditate on the authority given to you by Jesus' life, death, and resurrection. Allow the Holy Spirit to fill you afresh and declare to you the purposes he has for you today. Commit yourself to being a minister of the Lord in every circumstance today and discover the incredible life available to you in the restoration of authority given to you by your heavenly Father.

GUIDED PRAYER

1. Meditate on the authority given to you by Jesus' life, death, and resurrection. Allow Scripture to renew your mind to the power and authority you have in the Spirit.

"I will give you the keys of the kingdom of heaven, and whatever you bind on earth shall be bound in heaven, and whatever you loose on earth shall be loosed in heaven." Matthew 16:19

"The seventy-two returned with joy, saying, 'Lord, even the demons are subject to us in your name!' And he said to them, 'I saw Satan fall like lightning from heaven. Behold, I have given you authority to tread on serpents and scorpions, and over all the power of the enemy, and nothing shall hurt you. Nevertheless, do not rejoice in this, that the spirits are subject to you, but rejoice that your names are written in heaven.'" Luke 10:17-20

2. Allow the Holy Spirit to fill you afresh and declare to you the purposes he has for you today. Ask him to give you revelation throughout your day on what he wants you to bind and loose on earth and in heaven.

3. Commit yourself to being a minister of the Lord in every circumstance today. Ask the Holy Spirit to empower you to live courageously and under his influence. Ask him to fill you with love and grace for others and to help you guide others into the fullness of relationship with their Creator.

"But God, being rich in mercy, because of the great love with which he loved us, even when we were dead in our trespasses, made us alive together with Christ— by grace you have been saved—and raised us up with

him and seated us with him in the heavenly places in Christ Jesus, so that in the coming ages he might show the immeasurable riches of his grace in kindness toward us in Christ Jesus." Ephesians 2:4-7

How abundant is our God's grace that he would choose to use us to advance his kingdom. How near is he to us that he longs to help us be reflections of his love in every circumstance. There is no greater life than one lived in pursuit of bringing God's kingdom to earth in all we do. There is no greater purpose than being used by the Holy Spirit to accomplish works of eternal significance. May you live today in light of the authority restored to you by the powerful sacrifice of Jesus.

Extended Reading: Matthew 16

Having Grace
for Others

DEVOTIONAL

In response to the wealth of grace given to us by our heavenly Father, we are called to be ministers of his grace to others. Until we set others free from having to live up to our standards, we will never experience true freedom ourselves. Living apart from an attitude of continual grace robs us of the joy of living without unrealistic expectations of others. When we are slow to offer grace for the sins of others, we step outside the realm of God's kingdom and place our hope and security in this fleeting world.

"A new commandment I give to you, that you love one another: just as I have loved you, you also are to love one another. By this all people will know that you are my disciples, if you have love for one another."

JOHN 13:34-35

Jesus tells an important story for us to heed in Matthew 18:21-35. In this parable a servant is forgiven of an insurmountable debt owed to the king. But rather than taking the grace he was shown and offering it to others, the servant sought out a fellow servant and began to choke him until he paid his debt. Upon hearing of his servant's lack of grace, the king has him thrown in prison until he paid off what he owed. And in verse 35 Jesus concludes, *"So also my heavenly Father will do to every one of you, if you do not forgive your brother from your heart."*

We are called to offer grace to others, and not because of who they are or what they've done. If grace were based on merit or self-worth, it wouldn't be grace. We are called to offer grace because no debt owed to us compares to the insurmountable debt of sin forgiven by the death of Jesus. There is no wrong someone could ever commit against us that could compare to the amount of unmerited favor we've received.

In showing grace to others we begin to experience to greater depths the joy of our heavenly Father. In offering mercy to the undeserving we shine the light of God's grace into the darkness of a world without second chances. May we not be like the unforgiving servant in Matthew 18, but instead be like our loving Savior. May we not conform to the patterns of unforgiveness found all around us, but instead cast our hope on heaven and let go of that which the world would deem rightfully ours. May we commit scandals of grace that the lost cannot comprehend and the world cannot explain. May the love of our heavenly Father shine through us as we run out to meet the weak and sinful at their point of need and offer them mercy and compassion.

1 Corinthians 13:1-3 says, *"If I speak in the tongues of men and of angels, but have not love, I am a noisy gong or a clanging cymbal. And if I have prophetic powers, and understand all mysteries and all knowledge, and if I have all faith, so as to remove mountains, but have not love, I am nothing. If I give away all I have, and if I deliver up my body to be burned, but have not love, I gain nothing."* May we gain everything as we seek to love others with God's compassion and grace. May we love beyond what the world understands and offer grace beyond what anyone could expect. Take time in guided prayer to allow God to fill you with a fresh revelation of the grace you've been shown. Allow your Father to fill you with his heart for others. And ask the Holy Spirit to transform you into a minister of his divine grace today.

GUIDED PRAYER

1. Allow God to fill you with a fresh revelation of his limitless grace. Meditate on Scripture and allow it to fill your heart with thanksgiving at how compassionate your heavenly Father is.

"For by grace you have been saved through faith. And this is not your own doing; it is the gift of God, not a result of works, so that no one may boast." Ephesians 2:8-9

"So that being justified by his grace we might become heirs according to the hope of eternal life." Titus 3:7

"For God so loved the world, that he gave his only Son, that whoever believes in him should not perish but have eternal life." John 3:16

2. Ask your heavenly Father to fill you with his heart for others. Ask him to whom he wants to offer grace through you today. Ask him how you can reveal his love and compassionate heart to the lost around you.

"In the same way, let your light shine before others, so that they may see your good works and give glory to your Father who is in heaven." Matthew 5:16

3. Ask the Holy Spirit to transform you into a minister of his divine grace. Ask him to give you the courage and perspective to love, forgive, and show grace to the undeserving.

"And God is able to make all grace abound to you, so that having all sufficiency in all things at all times, you may abound in every good work." 2 Corinthians 9:8

The father in the parable of the prodigal son didn't hesitate to show his rebellious child grace. He ran out to meet him at his point of greatest need and restored him to the life for which he had been born. Don't hesitate to show grace today. Don't wait to be used by your heavenly Father. Run out to meet those who are at their lowest points. Affirm and encourage those who have given up on themselves. Love and restore those who feel shame and helplessness. May your heavenly Father use you in powerful ways to reveal his loving grace to a world in desperate need of unmerited mercy.

Extended Reading: Matthew 18

Poor in spirit

"Blessed are the poor in spirit, for theirs is the kingdom of heaven."
Matthew 5:3

WEEKLY OVERVIEW

The biblical concept of being poor in spirit is foundational to every aspect of the Christian life. Foundational to salvation is a heart-level acknowledgment of our need for a Savior. Foundational to experiencing God's love is acknowledging our great need of love. Foundational to heavenly peace and joy is an acknowledgment that this world truly offers us neither. If we want all that God in his grace offers, we must pursue a lifestyle of being poor in spirit. May you experience more of the depth of God's love this week as you discover God's heart to minister to those desperate for him.

Poor in Spirit

DEVOTIONAL

"Blessed are the poor in spirit, for theirs is the kingdom of heaven" (Matthew 5:3). Who is this God that he would bless those who are spiritually impoverished with the greatest gift of all: the kingdom of heaven? Our God demonstrated his wealth of grace, help, and love to all who were in need through the words and actions of Jesus. Jesus, who came to reveal the heart of the Father, was undoubtedly drawn to the weak, desperate, and estranged. And in comparison to his affection for the impoverished he was incredibly critical of all those enveloped with mankind's chief sin: pride.

Jesus' ministry made clear what thousands of years of religion, sin, and the rule of the law obscured: the necessity of being poor in spirit to have true relationship with God. You see, even today we buy into a false doctrine that our works somehow justify us to God. Even today we believe that we must clean ourselves up, do better, work harder, or love more to have relationship with our heavenly Father. Jesus came to obliterate works-based relationship and to reveal God's heart of unconditional, grace-filled, unchanging, and system-shattering love.

Jesus powerfully illustrates this truth in Luke 18:9-14. May his words shed light on any part of our hearts that still believe we must do something to deserve the affections of a loving Father:

He also told this parable to some who trusted in themselves that they were righteous, and treated others with contempt: "Two men went up into the temple to pray,

*"God opposes the proud, but
gives grace to the humble."*

JAMES 4:6

one a Pharisee and the other a tax collector. The Pharisee, standing by himself, prayed thus: 'God, I thank you that I am not like other men, extortioners, unjust, adulterers, or even like this tax collector. I fast twice a week; I give tithes of all that I get.' But the tax collector, standing far off, would not even lift up his eyes to heaven, but beat his breast, saying, 'God, be merciful to me, a sinner!' I tell you, this man went down to his house justified, rather than the other. For everyone who exalts himself will be humbled, but the one who humbles himself will be exalted."

Your Father loves you because he loves you. He longs to exalt you. He longs to bless you. He longs to pour out the full extent of his loving-kindness over every possible area of your life. But to reward you for a works-based mentality is to reinforce behavior that will only harm you. It's only in acknowledging your total and utter dependency on God that you will be able to receive the depth of his love. It's only in serving him because you are loved, rather than to be loved, that your works will yield heavenly fruit. It's only in being poor in spirit that you will discover yourself already perfectly and completely loved, liked, and enjoyed. You will then experience the freedom and joy that comes from uninhibited relationship with God's limitless love.

Take time in guided prayer to search out the true condition of your heart. Ask the Holy Spirit to illuminate any part of your life that is works-based rather than grace-based. Be honest with yourself and God that the fullness of your need would be met with the fullness of his love for you.

GUIDED PRAYER

1. Meditate on the importance of being poor in spirit. Allow Scripture to ignite in you a pursuit of consistently acknowledging your need.

"For thus says the One who is high and lifted up, who inhabits eternity, whose name is Holy: 'I dwell in the high and holy place, and also with him who is of a contrite and lowly spirit, to revive the spirit of the lowly, and to revive the heart of the contrite.'" Isaiah 57:15

"All these things my hand has made, and so all these things came to be, declares the Lord. But this is the one to whom I will look: he who is humble and contrite in spirit and trembles at my word." Isaiah 66:2

"Blessed are the poor in spirit, for theirs is the kingdom of heaven." Matthew 5:3

2. Ask the Holy Spirit to help you think of any ways in which you are living a works-based life instead of a grace-based life. Where are you doing life in your own strength? Where are you working for the affection of God and others? Where are you striving for that which is already yours in Christ?

3. Take time to acknowledge your need before God. Be honest with the condition of your heart. Be honest with your sin and brokenness. Receive the love of God who gives it freely, not because you deserve it, but because he is good.

"For God so loved the world, that he gave his only Son, that whoever believes in him should not perish but have eternal life." John 3:16

"But God shows his love for us in that while we were still sinners, Christ died for us." Romans 5:8

"Can a woman forget her nursing child, that she should have no compassion on the son of her womb? Even these may forget, yet I will not forget you. Behold, I have engraved you on the palms of my hands; your walls are continually before me." Isaiah 49:15-16

"To be human is to be poor" (Brennan Manning, *The Ragamuffin Gospel*). All of us are broken. All of us are in need. The greatest symptom of our brokenness is not acknowledging it. It's only in pride that our need goes unmet. It's only in pride that our brokenness is without healing. We serve a good, loving Father who has always loved us. When we stop trying to prove to ourselves, God, and others that we have our lives together, we actually begin to truly live. There is overwhelming freedom, joy, and love in living with the reality that we are wholly accepted and loved just as we are. May you discover the abundant life available to you as you live poor in spirit.

Extended Reading: Psalm 51

Lifestyle of Grace

DAY 23

DEVOTIONAL

When we live poor in spirit we position ourselves to receive the limitless grace of our heavenly Father. To be poor in spirit is by definition to acknowledge our immense, total need of God's help. And throughout Scripture, God declares that his heart is for those who acknowledge their need of him. Isaiah 66:2 says, *"All these things my*

"All these things my hand has made, and so all these things came to be, declares the Lord. But this is the one to whom I will look: he who is humble and contrite in spirit and trembles at my word."

ISAIAH 66:2

hand has made, and so all these things came to be, declares the Lord. But this is the one to whom I will look: he who is humble and contrite in spirit and trembles at my word." God's grace is for those poor in spirit.

Paul demonstrated this truth in 2 Corinthians 12:9 where God told him, *"My grace is sufficient for you, for my power is made perfect in weakness."* And exhibiting the proper response to God's truth, Paul says, *"Therefore I will boast all the more gladly of my weaknesses, so that the power of Christ may rest upon me."* I long for the power of Christ in my life. I long to live entirely by his perfect grace. And Scripture declares to you and me today that the way we access the fullness of God's grace is by living poor in spirit. We must open our eyes to see the true state of our spiritual health, not in comparison to others, but in comparison to Jesus. And we must allow a revelation of our spiritual depravity to lead us to a continual acknowledgement of our need of God's grace.

The truth is that to be anything but poor in spirit is to live under false pretense, to live a lie. Our humanity screams of our depravity. Our weaknesses are vast and plainly visible. But society tells us we need to work to cover up our mess. Even the church often values appearance above reality. Rather than being a hospital to the weak, needy, and spiritually depraved, church is often a club where only those who speak the lingo, dress accordingly, smell nice, and never speak of their problems feel welcome.

"Blessed are the poor in spirit, for theirs is the kingdom of heaven" (Matthew 5:3). Fitting in to the cliques of this world is nothing in comparison to an abundant life filled with the limitless grace of God. Getting a slap on the back from the world for looking like I have it all together is nothing in comparison to the freedom of coming before God openly and honestly.

James 4:6 simply declares, *"God gives grace to the humble."* May we be those who have the courage to live honestly. May we have the courage to look at ourselves for who we truly are with all our faults, weaknesses, sin, pride, and immense need of help. And may we discover the wealth of life available only in the grace of an all-loving, sinner-accepting, and help-giving God.

GUIDED PRAYER

1. Meditate on the importance of being poor in spirit in receiving God's grace.

"All these things my hand has made, and so all these things came to be, declares the Lord. But this is the one to whom I will look: he who is humble and contrite in spirit and trembles at my word." Isaiah 66:2

"God opposes the proud, but gives grace to the humble." James 4:6

"But the tax collector, standing far off, would not even lift up his eyes to heaven, but beat his breast, saying, 'God, be merciful to me, a sinner!' I tell you, this man went down to his house justified, rather than the other. For everyone who exalts himself will be humbled, but the one who humbles himself will be exalted." Luke 18:13-14

2. Take an honest look at yourself. Take account of your thoughts, emotions, and actions. Compare the state of your life to the call of God to look like Jesus.

"As for me, I am poor and needy, but the Lord takes thought for me. You are my help and my deliverer; do not delay, O my God!" Psalm 40:17

3. Come before your loving heavenly Father openly and honestly declaring your need of his grace. Rest in his loving presence and let him reveal to you how deeply he enjoys you just as you are. Discover that his grace meets you at every point of need, sin, and weakness.

"My grace is sufficient for you, for my power is made perfect in weakness." 2 Corinthians 12:9

In 1 Corinthians 15:10 Paul says, *"But by the grace of God I am what I am, and his grace toward me was not in vain. On the contrary, I worked harder than any of them, though it was not I, but the grace of God that is with me."* To be poor in spirit is to accomplish far more than you ever could in your own strength. Being poor in spirit should never result in sluggishness or a lack of good works. Rather, it positions you to receive the grace of God whereby your works are of an eternal nature and filled with the anointing and power of your loving, near, heavenly Father. May you live today entirely by the grace of God and find the help of the Holy Spirit to be constant and tangible.

Extended Reading: Psalm 40

121

Repentance and God's Promised Forgiveness

DAY 24

DEVOTIONAL

In his book *The Ragamuffin Gospel*, Brennan Manning makes an incredibly astute observation of those who are poor in spirit. He writes, "The saved sinner is prostrate in adoration, lost in wonder and praise. He knows repentance is not what we do in order to earn

"In him we have redemption through his blood, the forgiveness of our trespasses, according to the riches of his grace."

EPHESIANS 1:7

forgiveness; it is what we do because we have been forgiven." To be poor in spirit is to live in a constant state of repentance founded on the already promised forgiveness of a just and loving God.

Ephesians 1:7 says, *"In him we have redemption through his blood, the forgiveness of our trespasses, according to the riches of his grace."* By the grace of God you and I are promised forgiveness every time we repent. We never have to question whether or not we have been forgiven. Every drop of Jesus' blood proved God's commitment both to justice and forgiveness. By the powerful sacrifice of Jesus, you and I have received reconciliation to a holy God, the greatest accomplishment of God's continual forgiveness.

If we are going to experience the fullness of life made available to us by God's continual forgiveness, we must seek to be poor in spirit. When we live as though we have it all together we blind ourselves to our continual need of repentance and forgiveness. When we compare our righteousness to other believers rather than God's command in 1 Peter 1:16, *"You shall be holy, for I am holy,"* we adopt a posture of being rich in spirit. To believe we are spiritually rich is to miss out on the continual provision of God to those who are in need. Not one of us is spiritually rich in and of ourselves. Not

one of us is without need of God's forgiveness. Not one of us can step outside of completely depending on God and live the life Jesus died to give us.

By contrast, those who live in a constant state of being poor in spirit experience the abundant joy and peace that comes from being wholly met by God's unconditional love. You and I don't have to clean ourselves up to come before our heavenly Father. We don't have to get our act together before we receive forgiveness for our sins. In fact, the quicker we turn to God in the middle of our mess the more we experience the ever-open arms of our heavenly Father running out to meet us (Luke 15:11-32).

There is joy in a holy, perfect God coming down to us at our greatest point of weakness. There is peace in knowing we are already accepted and loved by our heavenly Father. True life in the kingdom of God comes to those who respond with awe, reverence, humility, and an acknowledgment of their own depravity to God's open invitation to receive his forgiveness and grace. Open your eyes to see your great need of God's forgiveness and grace. Take an honest look at your life. And seek continual, immediate repentance for your sin knowing that you will always be met with instant forgiveness and compassion from the Father.

123

GUIDED PRAYER

1. Meditate on living a lifestyle of repentance from a place of God's promised forgiveness. Reflect on the availability of continual forgiveness for your sin. Allow Scripture to fill you with a desire to continually and immediately repent to your loving heavenly Father.

"If we confess our sins, he is faithful and just to forgive us our sins and to cleanse us from all unrighteousness." 1 John 1:9

"Let the wicked forsake his way, and the unrighteous man his thoughts; let him return to the Lord, that he may have compassion on him, and to our God, for he will abundantly pardon." Isaiah 55:7

"For you know the grace of our Lord Jesus Christ, that though he was rich, yet for your sake he became poor, so that you by his poverty might become rich." 2 Corinthians 8:9

2. Take an honest look at yourself. Where do you have sin? What parts of your life are in desperate need of God's help? Where are you not living holy as your heavenly Father is holy?

"You shall be holy, for I am holy." 1 Peter 1:16

"If we say we have no sin, we deceive ourselves, and the truth is not in us." 1 John 1:8

3. Ask the Holy Spirit to help you live in a continual state of need today. Take time to rest in his forgiveness and accept your need of his grace. Place yourself in the prodigal son story and see the heart of God in the character of the father (see below in the extended reading).

"In him we have redemption through his blood, the forgiveness of our trespasses, according to the riches of his grace." Ephesians 1:7

To live in a constant state of repentance and receiving forgiveness is to live free from the weight of worldliness. There is joy in repentance. There is life in reconciliation. David declares in Psalm 40:1-3,

"I waited patiently for the Lord; he inclined to me and heard my cry. He drew me up from the pit of destruction, out of the miry bog, and set my feet upon a rock, making my steps secure. He put a new song in my mouth, a song of praise to our God."

We live in the security of God's unconditional love and forgiveness when we seek a lifestyle of repentance. May you discover the joy and peace available to you in the heart of God to show you grace and mercy in your weakness and repentance.

Extended Reading: 1 John 1

124

Seeking Wealth in Heaven

DEVOTIONAL

To be poor in spirit is to seek wealth in heaven rather than in the things of the world. Jesus says in Matthew 5:3, *"Blessed are the poor in spirit, for theirs is the kingdom of heaven."* We have no reason to be poor in spirit if we're after the world. The world does not reward those who acknowledge their weaknesses. The world does not revere and honor those who are open and honest about their brokenness. But God says in Proverbs 29:23, *"One's pride*

"But seek first the kingdom of God and his righteousness, and all these things will be added to you."

MATTHEW 6:33

will bring him low, but he who is lowly in spirit will obtain honor." Seeking wealth in heaven and honor from the One, True God requires us to live in light of the fact that we are dust. God rewards only those who obey his command to be poor in spirit.

Scripture is clear that our actions here on earth affect our eternal life. Jesus says in Matthew 6:19-21, 24,

"Do not lay up for yourselves treasures on earth, where moth and rust destroy and where thieves break in and steal, but lay up for yourselves treasures in heaven, where neither moth nor rust destroys and where thieves do not break in and steal. For where your treasure is, there your heart will be also. . . . No one can serve two masters, for either he will hate the one and love the other, or he will be devoted to the one and despise the other. You cannot serve God and money."

What Jesus is not saying in Matthew 6 is that we are not to have any form of money here on earth. God knows our needs, and in the very next section of Scripture he tells us not to fear for them because he promises to provide (Matthew 6:31-32). What he is saying is summed up in in Matthew 6:33, *"But seek first the kingdom of God and his righteousness, and all these things will be added to you."*

To be poor in spirit on earth is to be rich in heaven. God honors and blesses those who live according to his commands rather than seeking pleasure in the world. Psalm 113:7-8 says, *"He raises the poor from the dust and lifts the needy from the ash heap, to make them sit with princes, with the princes of his people."* When we seek earthly wealth, it dies with us. But when we live in truth, acknowledging that we are dust and that all the worldly pursuits are fleeting and folly, all that's left is to give our heart to God.

Take time today to assess whether you are pursuing the things of the world or if your heart is solely devoted to God's kingdom. Assess whether you are seeking fulfillment for your spiritual need or attempting to fill the voids in your life with earthly success. And commit your heart to the Lord alone that you might receive heavenly reward that will satisfy you for all eternity. God longs to bless his children. He longs to provide abundantly for all your needs both here on earth and in heaven. But the gateway to both is narrow and requires you to be poor in spirit. May your heart be entirely God's today as you seek satisfaction and provision in him alone.

127

GUIDED PRAYER

1. Meditate on the value of seeking the kingdom of God above all else. Allow Scripture to inform the posture of your heart toward being poor in spirit.

"Do not lay up for yourselves treasures on earth, where moth and rust destroy and where thieves break in and steal, but lay up for yourselves treasures in heaven, where neither moth nor rust destroys and where thieves do not break in and steal. For where your treasure is, there your heart will be also." Matthew 6:19–21

"But seek first the kingdom of God and his righteousness, and all these things will be added to you." Matthew 6:33

"Blessed are the poor in spirit, for theirs is the kingdom of heaven." Matthew 5:3

2. In what ways are you seeking the things of the world over the kingdom of God? In what ways are you attempting to appear spiritually rich rather than poor in spirit? In what ways are you seeking wealth here rather than in heaven?

"And when you pray, you must not be like the hypocrites. For they love to stand and pray in the synagogues and at the street corners, that they may be seen by others. Truly, I say to you, they have received their reward." Matthew 6:5

3. Take time to confess any pursuits of the world to God and receive his forgiveness. Ask him to show you how your work and relationships fit into seeking his kingdom first. Commit all your finances, friends, and family to him.

The Bible speaks so strongly about earthly wealth because it can be so tempting, and because it carries with it a false sense of satisfaction. It's so easy for our hearts to become wrapped up in the things of this world when they're readily available to us. Earthly success and wealth are so enticing. But if we make time to discover the wealth of affection, satisfaction, joy, peace, and purpose that are found in seeking God's kingdom alone, the things of this world begin to come into a correct perspective. What is wealth here in comparison to eternal reward given to us by God himself? What is worldly pleasure in comparison to honor and blessing from the King of kings? Make space to simply enjoy God today in order that all other pursuits might fall into place in light of his unconditional love and desire to bless you.

Extended Reading: Matthew 6

The Blessing of Spiritual Poverty

DAY 26

DEVOTIONAL

To be rich in spirit based on our own accomplishments is to bear the weight of our own spiritual growth. In comparison, when we acknowledge our spiritual poverty before God, thereby contributing all that we do and are to his limitless grace, the weight of our spirituality is lifted off and placed squarely on the shoulders of Jesus, where it belongs. To be spiritually poor is to be incredibly blessed.

I've spent much of my Christian life seeking to do good. I've gone to church, Bible studies, small groups, accountability groups, and have played in worship bands. I've gone on mission trips, fed the homeless, served at food pantries, given up sleep, spent nights out to invest in others, and even dedicated my career to God. But it seemed like with every good work I was

doing I had to continually look to the next. I couldn't take time to rest or enjoy God because the weight of my righteousness and the fruit of my life rested solely on my shoulders. I didn't know how to live by grace, so instead I filled every waking moment with a fight to do all I could on my own.

Now it's not that any of those works were inherently bad. In fact, I am continuing to do most of those things today. The difference is found in John 15:5-9 where Jesus says,

"I am the vine; you are the branches. Whoever abides in me and I in him, he it is that bears much fruit, for apart from me you can do nothing. If anyone does not abide in me he is thrown away like a branch and withers; and the

> *"I dwell in the high and holy place, and also with him who is of a contrite and lowly spirit, to revive the spirit of the lowly, and to revive the heart of the contrite."*
>
> **ISAIAH 57:15**

branches are gathered, thrown into the fire, and burned. If you abide in me, and my words abide in you, ask whatever you wish, and it will be done for you. By this my Father is glorified, that you bear much fruit and so prove to be my disciples. As the Father has loved me, so have I loved you. Abide in my love."

When we live in acknowledgement of our immense need for God's help, we place ourselves on the path to abiding. Just as a sheep cannot find food, shelter, or water without abiding in the help of a shepherd, we are in immense need of our Good Shepherd. Problems arise when we see ourselves as more than helpless sheep and try to go our own way by living in our own strength. Pride covers up our true state of need. Being poor in spirit opens our eyes to see our true state of helplessness and helps us lean on the ever ready, capable, and available help of our good and faithful Father.

"For thus says the One who is high and lifted up, who inhabits eternity, whose name is Holy: 'I dwell in the high and holy place, and also with him who is of a contrite and lowly spirit, to revive the spirit of the lowly, and to revive the heart of the contrite'" (Isaiah 57:15). May your day be blessed by abiding in a God who is *"high and lifted up, who inhabits eternity, whose name is Holy,"* but is *"with him who is of a contrite and lowly spirit."* May your spiritual poverty lead you to a life filled with the glorious, incomprehensible presence, grace, and love of your Good Shepherd. And may you abide in the loving arms of your heavenly Father as he wholly enriches your life with his loving-kindness.

GUIDED PRAYER

1. Meditate on the blessing of being spiritually poor. Allow Scripture to fill you with courage to look at the state of your life and acknowledge your need of God.

"For thus says the One who is high and lifted up, who inhabits eternity, whose name is Holy: 'I dwell in the high and holy place, and also with him who is of a contrite and lowly spirit, to revive the spirit of the lowly, and to revive the heart of the contrite.'" Isaiah 57:15

"Blessed are the poor in spirit, for theirs is the kingdom of heaven." Matthew 5:3

"But he said to me, 'My grace is sufficient for you, for my power is made perfect in weakness.' Therefore I will boast all the more gladly of my weaknesses, so that the power of Christ may rest upon me." 2 Corinthians 12:9

2. Where have you been living life in your own strength? Where is your life not marked by the fruit of abiding in God's grace and presence?

"I am the vine; you are the branches. Whoever abides in me and I in him, he it is that bears much fruit, for apart from me you can do nothing. If anyone does not abide in me he is thrown away like a branch and withers; and the branches are gathered, thrown into the fire, and burned. If you abide in me, and my words abide in you, ask whatever you wish, and it will be done for you. By this my Father is glorified, that you bear much fruit and so prove to be my disciples. As the Father has loved me, so have I loved you. Abide in my love." John 15:5-9

3. Take time to cast the weight of your spirituality on the shoulders of your Good Shepherd. Abide in the love of your heavenly Father. Allow him to take the weight of all you've been working toward and replace it with the joy of simply knowing him.

"Humble yourselves, therefore, under the mighty hand of God so that at the proper time he may exalt you, casting all your anxieties on him, because he cares for you." 1 Peter 5:6-7

"As for me, I am poor and needy, but the Lord takes thought for me. You are my help and my deliverer; do not delay, O my God!" Psalm 40:17

133

It is a process to learn to bear fruit out of abiding in God. It's a place of trust to begin good works by simply enjoying the love of your Father. But Scripture is clear that it is only in resting in the grace and help of our Shepherd that we will bear any form of good fruit. God has good works in store for you that will extend far past the reach of this life. He has an amazing plan to use you to bring his kingdom to earth all around you. But the blessing of making a deep and lasting impact all begins by continually enjoying the love of a good God who would come down to meet you even in your weakness, need, and sin. Rest in the love of your Father today and allow him to plant desires in you that he will come and fulfill by his limitless grace.

Extended Reading: John 15

How to Live Low

DEVOTIONAL

All throughout Scripture God paints a clear picture of what it looks like to live poor in spirit—to live low. As we dive into the depths of God's word, I pray our lives will begin to be molded and shaped by the capable, loving hands of our Potter. I pray that we will look to the grace of God as our source and strength to pursue a lifestyle of humility. And I pray our lives will be enriched and blessed by the loving, powerful presence of a God who dwells with those who live low.

Philippians 2:3-7 says,

"Do nothing from rivalry or conceit, but in humility count others more significant than yourselves. Let each of you look not only to his own interests, but also to the interests of others. Have this mind among yourselves, which is

*"The reward for humility and fear of the
Lord is riches and honor and life."*

PROVERBS 22:4

*yours in Christ Jesus, who, though he was in the form of
God, did not count equality with God a thing to be grasped,
but made himself nothing, taking the form of a servant,
being born in the likeness of men."*

Living low always begins by looking at the life of Jesus. He is the author and perfecter of our faith (Hebrews 12:2). He is the example of what it looks like to live perfectly by the grace of the Father in a lifestyle of humble surrender. And Scripture makes it clear that he is our standard. A life like his is the goal.

Jesus, although King of kings and Lord of lords, did everything out of total love for God and man. The only man to ever live a perfect life looked to the interests of others above his own. One of the most powerful depictions of his commitment to loving those in need at all costs is found in Mark 2:13-17, where Jesus ate with tax collectors and sinners. Jesus loved others at the continual sacrifice of his reputation. He lived without a care of how he was perceived by man because his life was continually laid down to the will of his heavenly Father alone. To live in the will of God will always cost us our pride. Pride and God's will are in direct opposition.

God is calling us to a lifestyle of love. To be poor in spirit is to *"count others more significant than yourselves."* A common misconception in living low

is that we must try and find ways that we are worse than others. God is not about comparison. His ways are not like ours. Rather, he is calling us to stop looking to ourselves at all and solely look to the significance of others. Jesus knew he was sinless. He knew he was God. Still, he counted others more significant because of his love and grace. We don't have to pursue false humility to love others well. Rather, by the grace of God we must stop looking to our own needs, our own sense of pride and reputation, lay down our lives at the cross of Christ, and love as he has called us to love.

To live low is to look at the life of Jesus, look at our own lives, and acknowledge the differences, as well as obeying the command of Scripture to live like him. And in our inability we must come before our heavenly Father in full knowledge that we'll never be like Jesus on our own. We must seek to abide in him and receive his wealth of affection, love, and grace that we might bear fruit. If we seek to live low by ceasing to look to ourselves and instead look to God and others, we will always, unfailingly be empowered by God.

Take time in guided prayer to look at the life of Jesus, look at your own life, and receive the power of the Holy Spirit that comes from abiding in the love of your heavenly Father.

GUIDED PRAYER

1. Meditate on Jesus' commitment to humility and living low. Allow his life to be the example by which you live yours.

"Do nothing from rivalry or conceit, but in humility count others more significant than yourselves. Let each of you look not only to his own interests, but also to the interests of others. Have this mind among yourselves, which is yours in Christ Jesus, who, though he was in the form of God, did not count equality with God a thing to be grasped, but made himself nothing, taking the form of a servant, being born in the likeness of men." Philippians 2:3-7

2. In what ways are you living in pride? In what ways are you looking to your own interests above the interests of others? Where do you need to count others as more significant than yourself?

3. Take time to abide in God's love. Ask the Holy Spirit to help you yield your life to him that you might bear the fruit of his dwelling within you. Look to God as your source and supply rather than your own strength. And live today in a constant pursuit of living low.

"As the Father has loved me, so have I loved you. Abide in my love." John 15:9

"Put on then, as God's chosen ones, holy and beloved, compassionate hearts, kindness, humility, meekness, and patience, bearing with one another and, if one has a complaint against another, forgiving each other; as the Lord has forgiven you, so you also must forgive." Colossians 3:12-13

"For by the grace given to me I say to everyone among you not to think of himself more highly than he ought to think, but to think with sober judgment, each according to the measure of faith that God has assigned." Romans 12:3

Proverbs 22:4 says, *"The reward for humility and fear of the Lord is riches and honor and life."* When you humble yourself before God and man, the pressure of finding your own joy, success, provision, and worth falls off and is replaced with the peace, love, security, and grace of your heavenly Father. Living low does not mean you will be without joy, peace, or possessions. Rather, it positions you to receive all the incredible fullness of heaven your good Father longs to give. Live low today and rid yourself of the weight of pride so that the foundation for your emotions, thoughts, and actions would be the love of a good, present, and powerful God.

Extended Reading: Philippians 2

Freedom in Spiritual Poverty

DAY 28

DEVOTIONAL

There is abundant freedom from sin available to those who in humility and acknowledgement of their brokenness look to God for help. God's heart is for freedom. He came, died, and rose again that we might no longer be entangled to the burdens of this world but be set free to experience the fullness of heaven on earth.

"Live as people who are free, not using your freedom as a cover-up for evil, but living as servants of God."

1 PETER 2:16

Isaiah 61:1 foretold of Jesus' purposes on the earth in saying, *"The Spirit of the Lord God is upon me, because the Lord has anointed me to bring good news to the poor; he has sent me to bind up the brokenhearted, to proclaim liberty to the captives, and the opening of the prison to those who are bound."* Through the powerful sacrifice of Jesus in living and dying for us, we have been set free.

But the Bible is clear that walking in the freedom made available by the blood of Jesus only happens as we continually yield our lives to him on a daily basis. Romans 6:7 and 11 say, *"For one who has died has been set free from sin. . . . So you also must consider yourselves dead to sin and alive to God in Christ Jesus."* 1 Peter 2:16 says, *"Live as people who are free, not using your freedom as a cover-up for evil, but living as servants of God."* And Galatians 5:13 says, *"For you were called to freedom, brothers. Only do not use your freedom as an opportunity for the flesh, but through love serve one another."* We experience continual freedom as we submit our lives to the purposes, presence, and plans of our heavenly Father.

There is freedom for you and me today if we will choose to live poor in spirit. Jesus set us free, not that we would continue to live for ourselves and the world, but that we would experience the abundant life that comes through humility and submission to our loving God. The Godhead continually models submission and humility. They continually serve one another in an irreconcilable paradox of being three and one. And God is calling us to follow his model.

Where are you struggling with the bonds of sin today? Where does the world seem to have a hold on you? Submit your life to the capable hands of your loving heavenly Father and ask him to reveal to you the path to freedom. Look for any parts of your life in which you are still living for yourself and the things of the world. There is no freedom available to us in the pursuits of the world. The abundant life found in God is in direct opposition to the ways and cares of the earth. Choose today to pursue the life God has laid before you, find your enjoyment in his loving nearness, and receive the freedom that comes from abiding in the presence of the Holy Spirit.

139

GUIDED PRAYER

1. Meditate on the connection between humility and freedom. Reflect on the opposition between the things of the world and abundant life in God.

"For one who has died has been set free from sin. . . . So you also must consider yourselves dead to sin and alive to God in Christ Jesus." Romans 6:7,11

"Live as people who are free, not using your freedom as a cover-up for evil, but living as servants of God." 1 Peter 2:16

"For you were called to freedom, brothers. Only do not use your freedom as an opportunity for the flesh, but through love serve one another." Galatians 5:13

2. Where are you not experiencing the freedom available to you in Christ? In what ways are you living for yourself and the world?

3. Take time to rest in the presence of God and ask him for his path to freedom for you. Submit the entirety of your life to him and listen for his voice. Ask him to reveal his love and grace to you that you might live empowered by his presence.

"Now the Lord is the Spirit, and where the Spirit of the Lord is, there is freedom." 2 Corinthians 3:17

"The Spirit of the Lord God is upon me, because the Lord has anointed me to bring good news to the poor; he has sent me to bind up the brokenhearted, to proclaim liberty to the captives, and the opening of the prison to those who are bound." Isaiah 61:1

"You have been set free from sin and have become slaves to righteousness." Romans 6:18 (NIV)

May the words of Romans 8:1-4 fill you with faith to seek the total freedom from sin available to you in God. May your day today be marked by victory over the enemy and his schemes. And may your life be filled with the peace and joy that comes from experiencing freedom from the burdens and cares of sin:

"There is therefore now no condemnation for those who are in Christ Jesus. For the law of the Spirit of life has set you free in Christ Jesus from the law of sin and death. For God has done what the law, weakened by the flesh, could not do. By sending his own Son in the likeness of sinful flesh and for sin, he condemned sin in the flesh, in order that the righteous requirement of the law might be fulfilled in us, who walk not according to the flesh but according to the Spirit."

Extended Reading: Romans 6

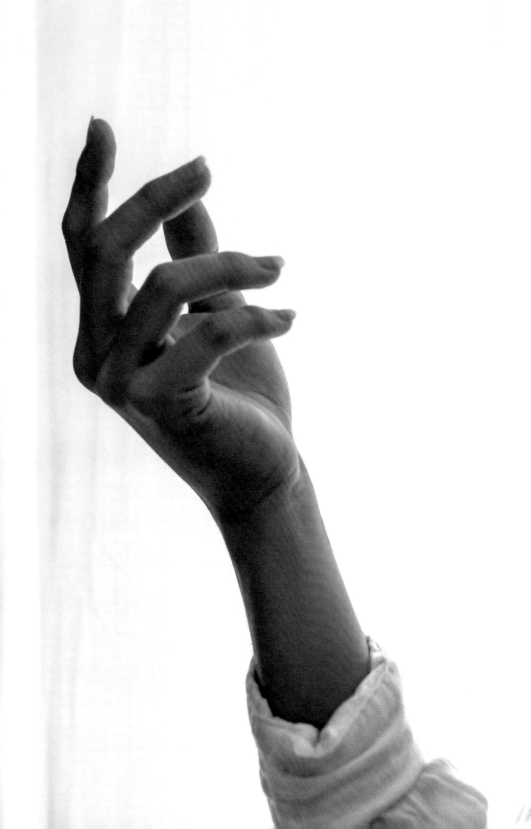